Revelation:
A Study of End-Time Events

Donna Best

To my loving and patient husband,
Larry, who has always encouraged me
in my assignments from the Lord.

CONTENTS

◆◆◆◆

LESSON ONE: INTRODUCTION & CHAPTER 1......................................1

LESSON TWO: CHAPTERS 2-3 15

LESSON THREE: CHAPTERS 4-5-6..................................28

LESSON FOUR: CHAPTERS 7-8-9..................................39

LESSON FIVE: CHAPTERS 10-11 48

LESSON SIX: CHAPTER 12 58

LESSON SEVEN: CHAPTER 13 68

LESSON EIGHT: CHAPTERS 14-15-16 76

LESSON NINE: CHAPTER 17 85

LESSON TEN: CHAPTER 18..................................96

LESSON ELEVEN: CHAPTERS 19-20..................................105

LESSON TWELVE: CHAPTERS 21-22 113

BIBLIOGRAPHY 125

LESSON ONE: INTRODUCTION & CHAPTER 1

◆◆◆◆

John on the Isle of Patmos

This study is a compilation of cross-references to other passages in the Bible that will shed light on the prophecies in Revelation, allowing Scripture to interpret Scripture. We are each responsible to test everything against the Word of God.

For small group study, no teacher is required. One person may read the lesson, with others sharing the reading of the Revelation verses, as well as the other passages as referenced. In fact, what we refer to as the "book" of Revelation was a letter circulated to the churches and usually read aloud by the pastor of the church.

Let the Holy Spirit guide you as you simply share in the reading of God's Word. You will not lack for discussion. To aid you in your study, discussion questions have been included at the end of every lesson. When there is a question, make it your assignment to search the Scriptures for your answers. While you will not learn all there is to know about the book of Revelation through this study, you will learn far more than you ever imagined. May God richly bless you as you study His Word.

I.   Introduction

        Have you been afraid to read the book of Revelation? One friend said her father had frightened her as a child when he talked about it. Another friend thought the writer (the apostle John) must have been on drugs! I can assure you that he was not. Just for a moment, put yourself in his place. He was trying to describe things he had never seen before with the language of his day. What might be the result?

Let's say that John saw a helicopter, and was trying to describe it based on his own experience and the knowledge of his day: "It looks like a giant locust with wings on its head and tail, and (if he saw the pilot) the face of a man!" Really scary, right? That is, in fact, similar to some of the descriptions in this book.

You may have heard of many things that come from the book of Revelation: The Four Horsemen of the Apocalypse...The Great Tribulation...The Antichrist (referred to as the "Beast") ...Armageddon. Do these things sound familiar?

A)   The book of Revelation is actually the unveiling of Jesus Christ in His glory and majesty, and the magnificent climax of world history —as it relates to Him.

B)   This study will give you a basic understanding of the book of Revelation in order to dispel your fears and confusion.

In fact, did you know that a blessing is conferred on anyone who reads this book and takes it to heart? We'll see that promise in our study of Chapter 1.

C)   This study guide presents a panoramic view of end-times prophecy:

1)   It will highlight major events and figures. We will see a sequence of events. We will not set dates.

2)   It will give you a desire to study God's Word in greater depth.

a)   We must let Scripture interpret Scripture. God's Word is a treasure, and we are on a treasure hunt.

b)   Much of the symbolism of Revelation is explained in the book of Daniel and elsewhere in the Bible.

    c)   We will look at other passages of Scripture that shed light on what we're reading in Revelation.

For example, the "Rapture" is not covered in Revelation, so we'll need to look elsewhere in Scripture to understand its meaning, since it is an essential aspect of the end times.

    D)   So…would you read a good book and stop just before the final chapter? Why not? You want to see how the story ends!

Have people told you that Revelation cannot be understood?

> *Any interpretation of the book of Revelation that discourages a believer from studying it, or a pastor from teaching it, is not the correct interpretation!*

How can we know this is a true statement?

"All Scripture is God-breathed and is useful for teaching, rebuking, correcting and training in righteousness, so that the man of God may be thoroughly equipped for every good work" (2 Tim. 3:16-17).

    1)   We will be interpreting the words of this prophecy based on Revelation 1:19, where John was told, "Write, therefore, what you have seen, what is now, and what will take place later."

        That word "later" in the Greek (*meta*) means *after*—after what is now. We will see that most of what occurs in the book of Revelation is in the future.

    2)   Scripture is not understood primarily through our intellect but, rather, truth is revealed to us by the Holy Spirit.

> *Therefore, always begin your study of God's Word with prayer.*

II. Background (generally accepted history):

A) <u>Author</u>: Traditionally held to be the apostle John, who also wrote one of the Gospels, and three letters.

B) <u>Place</u>: The book of Revelation, which was in the form of a letter circulated to seven churches in the same region (modern-day Turkey), was written from the nearby Isle of Patmos.

C) <u>Date</u>: John was exiled by the Roman Emperor Domitian in AD 95 for preaching faith in Christ alone. (Domitian demanded that he be worshipped as a god). John was released soon after Domitian died in AD 96. It was during that brief period of time on the Isle of Patmos that John experienced and recorded The Revelation of Jesus Christ.

D) <u>Purpose</u>: While there was a future purpose in recording this prophecy, the immediate purpose in John's day was to encourage believers to hold fast to their faith. Some in the church at that time were advocating compromise in order to avoid persecution.[1]

　　1) What are some ways that we compromise in our culture to avoid persecution or rejection?

　　　　a) Silence our voice against sin?

　　　　b) Silence the gospel truth that Jesus is the only way to be reconciled with God the Father?

---

[1] *The NIV Study Bible, New International Version* ® (Grand Rapids, MI: Zondervan Publishing House, 1995), 1922. Introductory notes on *Revelation*. Used by permission.

2) Through John's vision, God is encouraging ALL believers to stand firm in the truth of Jesus Christ, in the midst of persecution, ridicule or rejection.

With all of Scripture, the writers were addressing believers during their day, about events of their day. Yet, there is a spiritual application for us today. Once we've determined what the writer said, and what he meant within the context of the passage, we can then make a spiritual application to our own lives.

Example:

2 Chronicles 7:14 "...If my people, who are called by my name, will humble themselves and pray and seek my face and turn from their wicked ways, then will I hear from heaven and will forgive their sin and will heal their land."

Here, the Lord was speaking to Solomon concerning the people of Israel, but it is so relevant to the Church today.

3) So, too, with the book of Revelation, all believers are encouraged by:

❖ The Revelation of Jesus Christ. Christ is revealed in glory, majesty, and victory at His second coming;

❖ Showing them (and us) the sovereign control of God in world events and the final outcome, without violating anyone's free will.

Shouldn't knowing that the Lord has control over the circumstances of our lives—and the chaos we are facing in our world today—give us a sense of peace and security?

III. Chapter One – Overview

We will see, in this first chapter, that the apostle John was exiled on the island of Patmos, where he received a vision from an angel: A Revelation of Jesus Christ. There is a blessing conferred on anyone who reads or hears, and takes to heart, what is in this vision. John is told to write what he sees, and he does so in a letter to seven nearby churches, in what is modern-day Turkey. Jesus Christ identifies Himself as the One who loves us and freed us from our sins by His blood.

At that point, we will need to step outside of the text of Revelation into other passages of Scripture that tell of the love story between the heavenly Bridegroom, Jesus Christ, and His Bride, the Church. The Church includes everyone who has trusted Christ as their Savior, both Jew and Gentile, since the birth of the Church at Pentecost. It is essential that we cover the passages dealing with the return of Christ for His Bride, at what is commonly referred to as the Rapture, so that it is not confused with His Second Coming, as described in <u>Revelation 1:7</u>. In fact, we will see in Chapter 19 that the Bride will return to earth with Christ.

In the vision, John saw and heard Christ speaking to him as He stood in dramatic appearance among seven lamp stands, later explained to be symbols of the seven churches. At this point, John is told to write what he has seen (Christ in glory, as Righteous Judge), what is now (the churches and Christ's messages to them), and what will take place later, in the future. It is in <u>Revelation 1:19</u> that we are told how to interpret the book itself.

Please turn to your Bible and read the passages in Revelation as indicated at the **left margin, in bold**. It is also essential that you read every verse or passage referenced. We will examine the Greek words used, since that was the language in which Revelation was written.

<u>1:1-2</u>

1) The Greek word for "revelation" is *apokalupsis*. Sound familiar? It should—it's the word from which we get "Apocalypse," which has come to mean the "end of the world." Actually, it is defined as "a disclosure of that which was previously hidden or unknown."[2] God, the Father, wants us to know about these coming events, as they relate to Jesus Christ, His Son.

---

[2] C.I. Scofield, ed., *The New Scofield Reference Bible, King James Version* (New York: Oxford University Press, 1967), 1351. Introductory notes on Revelation.

2) The word "soon" (*en tachei*) used here obviously doesn't mean right away because it was written 2,000 years ago. Instead, it means "quickly or suddenly coming to pass."[3] When it happens, it will happen suddenly.

1:3

1) The blessing here is promised to anyone who reads or hears, and takes to heart, what is written: to all believers of all time. Even an unbeliever will be blessed, for he may come to faith in Christ by it: "Faith comes by hearing...the word of Christ" (Rom. 10:17).

2) We are told that this time is near.

   a) Let's look at the meaning of the original Greek word for "time" (*kairos*): It refers to a "period of time."

   b) "Near" *(engus)* means "ready to take place at any time."

We will see in our study that this is "a period of time" (the return of Christ and the events leading up to that event) that is "ready to take place at any time," beginning with the Rapture of the Church. As we saw in verse 2, this period of time will come upon the world suddenly.

1:4-6

1) The seven churches mentioned here are both literal and symbolic. The number seven, as used in Scripture (54 times in Revelation), is commonly accepted as being symbolic of perfection or completion.

These seven churches are representative of the Church Age, which includes all true believers from Pentecost until the Rapture of the Church.

---

2) "seven Spirits" ("sevenfold spirit") speaks of the seven manifestations of the Holy Spirit in Isaiah 11:1-2.

---

[3] John Walvoord, *The Revelation of Jesus Christ* (Chicago: Moody Press, 1966), 35.

3)   The word "Trinity" is not found in Scripture, but is used to identify the three persons in One God (Father, Son and Holy Spirit). God is ONE in essence, character and perfection. Scripture tells us that Jesus is not only the Son of God. He IS God.

Read Philippians 2:5-7. Did you know that cults (false religions) deny that Jesus is God, and that He is the <u>only</u> begotten Son of God? He is not one of many gods!

4)   To Him who loves us:
        Jesus Christ is the Bridegroom, the Church is His Bride

---

At this point, we will step outside of the book of Revelation to look at other Scriptures that tell us of the Rapture of the Church, which is not to be confused with Christ's Second Coming.

Because the Church is the Bride of Christ (Eph. 5:22-31), for whom He is returning, it is essential that we understand the Old Testament wedding tradition. When sons married, they added onto their father's house as they prepared a home for their bride. The bride would prepare herself, not knowing exactly when her bridegroom would arrive to take her to his father's house. When the home was ready (and it was the father who determined this), the bridegroom would go to his bride and take her to the wedding ceremony and feast.

a)   Read John 14:1-6. Jesus is preparing a place for us.

b)   Read I Thessalonians 4:16-18. Christ will return for His Bride.

The dead in Christ will not be forgotten. Their souls are present in heaven (2 Cor. 5:8), will return with the Lord at the Rapture (1 Thess. 4:14-15), and will be reunited with their resurrected bodies at that time. Please read 1 Corinthians 15:51-54. Those who are still alive are "caught up" to be with the Lord in the air. (The word "rapture" comes from the Latin for "caught up"). This is the return of Christ for His Bride, which will include every believer since the birthing of the Church at Pentecost.

c) According to <u>1 Corinthians 15:51-52</u>, the Bride͜ caught up at the sounding of the last trumpet. This is nͨ of the trumpet judgments, as we will see in our study of Revelaͭͨ Just as the Old Testament Jewish Feast of Pentecost marked the birth of the Church in Acts 2, the Feast of Trumpets points to the Rapture of the Church.

d) <u>Read Rev. 19:6-8</u>. This passage refers to a future scene in heaven, immediately before Christ returns to earth at His Second Coming.

<u>Return to Revelation 1:7 – The Announcement of Christ's Second Coming</u>

1:7-8 This event is not the Rapture. At Christ's Second Coming, His Bride (the Church) will be with Him, as referenced in <u>19:6-8</u> above. Please read <u>Rev.19:14</u>, as well. The fine linen stands for the righteous acts of the saints.

Please keep your place here, and turn to the <u>Revelation Timeline – Ages Only</u> at the end of this lesson, to see a visual of the sequence of events.

Let's return to our passage in Revelation:

1:9-15

1) The symbolic meaning of the lampstands is given in v. 20. They are symbols for seven literal churches in John's day. Jesus is standing in their midst.

2) "Son of Man" is a reference to Christ in His humanity. Jesus is fully God and fully human. <u>Read John 3:13-16</u>.

When does a gift become ours? When we receive it.
Have you trusted Christ as your Savior and received the free gift of eternal life?

You will be given an opportunity to offer a simple prayer
for salvation at the close of this lesson.

1:16 A "double-edged sword" speaks of the Word of God.
1) <u>Read Hebrews 4:12.</u>

    a)   The word used for "sword" here (*machaira*) is defined as a "large knife for cutting flesh; small sword." It's the same word used in <u>Ephesians 6:17</u>: "Take the helmet of salvation and the sword of the Spirit, which is the Word of God."

    b)   The word "flesh" is also a biblical term that refers to our ego, will and appetites, when we are functioning independently of God. The sword of the Spirit, which is the Word of God, is used to cut away our "flesh" so that we may be conformed to Christ and walk under the Holy Spirit's control.

2) That is not the same Greek word used here, in <u>Rev. 1:16</u>, where "sword" is *rhomphaia*, "a large sword used as an instrument of judgment."

3) <u>Read Rev.19:15</u>. "Strike down" (*patasso*) is "to smite down, cut down, to kill, slay."

<u>1:17-18</u>
1) Believers have been delivered from God's wrath. <u>Read John 3:36.</u>

2) Christ holds the keys of death and Hades ("the realm of the dead").

Please keep your place here, and review the <u>Chart on Hades</u> at the end of this lesson before moving on to <u>Revelation 1:19</u> below.

<u>1:19</u> This verse is the key to interpreting the book of Revelation.

1) *What John has seen*: (Chapter 1) Christ in glory, as the Righteous Judge.

2) *What is now*: (Chapters 2 & 3) Christ's messages to specific churches of John's time and to all believers of the present "Church Age."

3) *What will take place later*: Later (*meta*) means "after" (after the Church Age, which will end with the Rapture of the Church). Chapters 4 through 22 are yet future.

> *The Church is never again mentioned on earth after Chapter 3.*
> *John is told, in Revelation 4:1, "Come up here, and*
> *I will show you what must take place after this."*

1:20 Here, we are told that the lampstands represent the churches, and the stars are "angels." The Greek word for "angels" here is *aggelos*, which means "a messenger, envoy, one who is sent, an angel, a messenger from God." John is told repeatedly in Chapters 2 and 3 to write these things to the angels (messengers) of these churches. He would not be writing to angelic beings, but rather to the pastors, who would read the messages to the believers in these churches.

> *If you now realize that you have never trusted Christ*
> *as your personal Savior, asking for His forgiveness,*
> *you can pray the following prayer of faith right now—*
> *and He will receive you as His own.*

Note to those in group studies: If you have already trusted Christ as your Savior, you can use this prayer as a profession of the faith you already possess, and walk side-by-side with those would come into God's kingdom today:

Lord Jesus, I believe that You are the only begotten Son of God, that You are fully God and fully human. I believe that You led a sinless life and that You died on the cross for the sins of the world—including mine. I believe that God the Father, by the power of the Holy Spirit, raised You from the dead, and that You will come again to judge the living and the dead. I ask you to forgive me and save me so that I can be reconciled with my Heavenly Father, be filled with the Holy Spirit, and live with You forever. I receive You as the Lord of my life and the Master of my soul. In Christ's Name, I pray. Amen.

Please refer to the Discussion Questions at the end of the lesson.

Revelation Timeline (Ages Only)

Church Age

Rapture of the Church

7-Year Tribulation

Divine Plan of Salvation

First Half of Tribulation: 3-1/2 years

The Church in Heaven

Revelation Chapters 4-19

Crowned Elders / Bride

Great Tribulation: 3-1/2 years

Return of Christ with His Bride

Millennium

Eternity

HADES

Before Christ died on the cross to pay the penalty for our sins:
Man died.... His soul went into Hades (Ex: Rich man and Lazarus: Luke 16: 19-31)

"Bosom of Abraham"
(Also called Paradise in Luke 23:39-43)

A place of peace and contentment where the souls of deceased Old Testament saints awaited Christ's death on the cross to pay the penalty for their sins.

****

Christ died on the cross to pay for our sins.
Matt. 12:40; Luke 23:39-43
****

Ascension of Christ (Acts 1:9): The souls of O.T. saints are led to heaven by Christ (Eph. 4:8-10); Paradise is now located in heaven (2 Cor. 12:2-4); NO LONGER IN HADES (Rev. 20:14).

****

At death, the believer's spirit goes immediately into the Lord's presence (2 Cor. 5:8), to await their physical resurrection and reward at the Rapture of the Church.

"Torment"
(Luke 16:23)

At death, the souls of ALL those who have rejected God's provision of salvation through Christ, enter "Hades" to await their final judgment before God.

****

After they are physically resurrected, they will stand before God to be judged. Then they will be cast—body and soul—into the Lake of Fire (Rev. 20:11-15).

****

When a lost person dies today, their soul goes to this place of torment. Since there is no longer a place in Hades for believers, "Hades" is now translated "Hell" by some scholars. However, the Greek word for "Hell" is "Gehenna," which speaks of the lake of fire, the final destination of the lost. No one has yet been cast into hell.

Revelation: A Study of End-Time Events Study Guide ©2007, 2019 Donna Best

Lesson One
Discussion Questions

Attention Small Group Leaders: Before proceeding to the following questions, please ask the members if there is a topic they want to discuss.

1)   What part of today's teaching was most important to you, and why?

2)   Please read the notes regarding the Rapture of the Church, beginning with Point #4 under <u>Revelation 1:4-6</u> (p. 8) of your study guide.

    a)   Is the Rapture of the Church a new concept to you?

    b)   What are some differences between the Rapture and the Second Coming of Christ, as described in <u>Revelation 1:7</u>?

    c)   Why do you think it is extremely important that we understand these distinctions?

3)   In <u>Revelation 1:19</u>, John is told to write down:

    ❖ What He has seen (Chapter 1: Christ as the Righteous Judge);
    ❖ What is now (Chapters 2-3: representing the Church Age); and
    ❖ What will take place later (Chapters 4-22: after the Church is raptured).

    Do you find this to be a valid method for interpreting the book of Revelation? If not, why not?

4)   Please refer to the Chart on Hades on p. 13 of your study guide. Was there any point in the Chart on Hades that you had never considered or been aware of before? Share what you learned.

LESSON TWO: CHAPTERS 2-3

◆◆◆◆

Messages to the Seven Churches

Overview

Each message to the churches is addressed to the "angel" of the church. But the Greek is *aggelos* which means "envoy, messenger, angel," and in this case, they are human messengers, most likely the pastor of each church. John would not have been writing to angelic beings.

In Chapters 2 and 3 we will see that John is told to write a specific message to each of the seven churches. Some churches receive Christ's commendation, others a rebuke, and some receive both. We will look at the reasons for each. But at the close of each of these seven messages, John is told to write:

"He who has an ear, let him hear what the Spirit is saying to the churches."

The messages were not just for one particular church, and neither was the Revelation itself. The entire letter (book) was meant to be circulated to all seven churches. There is a spiritual application for all believers. At the close of each message, Christ makes a promise "to him who overcomes." All believers overcome through faith in Christ.

Read 1 John 5:5 (same writer—John); Rev.12:11. How do we overcome?

The promises to the seven churches are different, yet applicable to all believers of all time, because we ALL overcome through faith in Christ. In this sense, these seven churches represent the entire Church, from Pentecost to the Rapture (the "Church Age"). In Scripture, the number seven is symbolic of perfection or completion. The order of the churches shows a historical progression towards the "hour of trial to come upon the whole world" (Rev. 3:10). Jesus spoke of this time of unequaled distress in Matthew 24:21.

The Church of Ephesus

2:1-5

1)   "You have forsaken your first love…." Christ Himself is our first love, our Savior. "Their warmth of love had given place to a lifeless orthodoxy."[4] Read Luke 7:36-47.

What is this woman demonstrating? Gratitude to her Savior. When we forget the magnitude of our sins, and the price Jesus paid for our salvation, our love for Him will grow cold. Here, the self-righteous Pharisee showed little love for Christ even though, in God's eyes, his sin was as offensive as the woman's. Even if we have "cleaned up our act" since becoming a Christian, we must always remember how much forgiveness we require.

2)   We know from Rev.1:20 that the lampstands represent the churches. Therefore, Jesus is telling them that if they don't repent, He'll remove their church, which was located in what is modern-day Turkey. Today, the country of Turkey is 98% Muslim.

2:6

1)   Who were the Nicolaitans and what were their practices? The word "Nicolaitans" (*Nikolaites*) means "destruction of people. The Nicolaitans abused the doctrine of salvation by grace to claim that sin was permitted, specifically foods offered to idols and sexual immorality."[5]

Read Romans 5:20-6:4

---

[4] Robert Jamieson, A.R. Fausset and David Brown, *Commentary Critical and Explanatory on the Whole Bible* (1871). Notes on Revelation 2:4. Public Domain.
[5] Ibid. Notes on Revelation 2:6.

<u>2:7</u>   Where have we read of the tree of life elsewhere in Scripture?

<u>Read Genesis 3:22</u>. Man was not allowed to eat from the tree of life after he had sinned, for he would have lived forever in that condition. God had another plan. This truth will have much to bear in the final chapters.

The Church in Smyrna

2:8-10

1)   Jesus promised that those who suffered persecution would receive "the crown of life." What does He mean by that? Is He speaking of eternal life?

   a)   The Greek definition of "crown" (*stephanos*), used here, is a "metaphor [of] the eternal blessedness which will be given as a prize to the genuine servants of God and Christ: the crown (wreath) which is the <u>reward</u> of the righteous."

   b)   This speaks of a "reward" (*misthose*), which means "wages earned; rewards God bestows on good deeds and endeavors."

   <u>Read Rev. 22:12</u>

   c)   We do not earn salvation/eternal life. It is not a reward; it is the gift of God. <u>Read Ephesians 2:8-9</u>.

   d)   The "crown of life" spoken of here is a reward for perseverance, in addition to the free gift of eternal life through faith in Christ.

2)   <u>There are five types of crowns mentioned in the New Testament as rewards for the saints:</u>

   ❖ The Crown of Life, for those who persevere under trials and persecution, even to the point of death (Rev. 2:10; James 1:12);

   ❖ The Crown of Righteousness, for those who have longed for His appearing (2 Tim. 4:8);

❖ The Crown of Glory, for those who faithfully serve the Church (1 Pet. 5:2-4);

❖ The Crown of Joy, for those who lead others to Christ (1 Thess. 2:19- 20);

❖ The Imperishable Crown, for those who have mastered their impulses and appetites, self-controlled as in the fruit of the Spirit (I Cor. 9:24-25).

2:11

1) Jesus promises that the overcomer (the believer) will not experience "the second death," which is the "lake of fire" (hell).

Read Rev. 20:11-15. This is the judgment of the wicked.

2) Believers' sins have already been judged on the cross. Instead, we will stand before the judgment (*bema*) seat of Christ, where our lives will be evaluated.

Read 2 Corinthians 5:10 and 1 Corinthians 3:12-15.

The Church in Pergamum

2:12-16

1) "Satan's seat—rather as the Greek is translated all through Revelation, 'throne.' Satan, in impious mimicry of God's heavenly throne, sets up his earthly throne. Æsculapius [the god of healing] was worshipped there under the serpent form, and Satan, the old serpent."[6]

2) In Rev. 2:14, we see another reference to idolatry and sexual immorality, practices that Jesus said He hated ("the practices of the Nicolaitans"). Balaam was a pagan prophet and sorcerer in the Old Testament. Balak, the King of Moab (enemies of Israel), summoned him and wanted him to put a curse on Israel (for money) so he could defeat them.

Balaam wanted the money, but God did not allow him to curse Israel.

---

[6] Jamieson, Fausset, Brown. Notes on Revelation 2:13.

Therefore, Balaam counseled Balak that if he could get the Israelites to fall into sin by intermarrying with heathen women, they could be led into idolatry and God would judge them Himself (Numbers 22-24, 31:15-16).

2:17

1) Manna was the type of food that the Lord provided for the Israelites in the desert ("manna" means "what is it?"). This is a reference to Christ as the Bread of Life. Read John 6:30-35.

2) What is the significance of the white stone? "In the ancient courts of justice, the accused were condemned by black pebbles, and acquitted by white."

The Church in Thyatira

2:18-21

1) The name "Jezebel" is probably used symbolically of the OT pagan Queen who was married to Israel's King Ahab, since she led her husband to forsake the Lord God and participate in idolatry (worship of idols), and the sexually immoral practices that involved.

2) (v. 21) The Greek word for "sexual immorality" is *porneia*. It means "illicit sexual intercourse; adultery, fornication, homosexuality, lesbianism, intercourse with animals etc., sexual intercourse with close relatives; Lev. 18." This is a direct quote from the Greek Lexicon.[7]

Read Genesis 2:18, 24.

a) (v. 24) "Man" (Hebrew "*iysh*") is defined in the Hebrew as "man, male, in contrast to woman, female. "Wife" (*ishshaw*) is "woman, wife, female, opposite of a man."[8] Also, read Matthew 19:4-5.

---

[7] Thayer and Smith, *New Testament Greek Lexicon.* Notes on Revelation 2:20. Public domain. Unless otherwise indicated, all Greek words and their meanings are taken from this text.

[8] Brown, Driver, Briggs and Gesenius. *Old Testament Hebrew Lexicon.* Notes on Gen. 2:24. Public domain. Unless otherwise indicated, all Hebrew words and their meanings are taken from this text.

b)   Therefore, sexual immorality includes heterosexual or homosexual sex outside of the one-man/one-woman marital union, including adultery (sex with one other than the spouse), pre-marital sex, living together without marriage, etc.

c)   Are there those in the Church today claiming that these practices are not sinful? Please read 2 Corinthians 10:3-5. The Greek word for "arguments" is *logismos*, which is an accounting term meaning "a reckoning, computation; reasoning, such as is hostile to the Christian faith."

When we reject the plain truth of God's Word, we are "adding up the facts" as we see them (human reasoning) and coming to a conclusion that is contrary to the Word of God. We then give that conclusion a higher value than the Word of God. Here, we are told that we are to "demolish" those arguments.

These are Jesus' own words to the Church.
While He hates the sinful and worldly practices of idolatry and
sexual immorality (Rev. 2:6), He loves the people committing them.
Our attitude should be like that of Christ Jesus.

---

3)   This union of one man/one woman is a picture, for all the world to see, of the spiritual relationship between Jesus Christ and His Bride, the Church.

4)   This "Jezebel" was leading believers astray into these immoral practices in the name of Christian freedom (same as the Nicolaitans). The word "misleads" *(planao)* means "to deceive; seduce."

Read 1 Corinthians 5:9-11.

2:22-25

1)   So much of our suffering is caused by our refusal to let go of our sin. The Jezebel in this church will reap what she has sown (Gal. 6:7).

2)   Her children (*teknon*) are "her proper adherents. In the NT, students or disciples are called children of their teachers because the latter, through their instruction, nourish the minds of their pupils, and mold their characters."[9]

3)   "Satan's so-called secrets" is likely a reference to Gnosticism ("full of knowledge"), a belief that one has special revelation from God about mysteries unknown by everyone else. BEWARE!

2:26-29

1)   We will share in Christ's authority, but the level of our authority will depend on our level of faithfulness in this life. Read Matthew 25:21, where Christ uses the parable of the talents to describe the kingdom of heaven.

2)   "I, Jesus [am]… the bright Morning Star" (Rev.22:16).

The Church in Sardis

3:1   "Dead" (*nekros*) is "destitute of force or power, inactive, inoperative."

3:2-4

1)   Jesus is speaking to a large unsaved population within the church (only a few are dressed in white/symbolic of Christ's righteousness credited to our account).

2)   "Soiled" (*moluno*) is defined as "to pollute, stain, contaminate, defile." Used here of those who have kept themselves "pure from the defilement of sin, and have not soiled themselves by fornication and adultery."

3)   "Walk" (*peripateo*) is "to conduct oneself." We have intimacy and fellowship with Christ when we walk in His ways, because He's not going to walk in ours!

3:5-6

1)   "Dressed in white…" Read Rev. 7:14.

---

[9] Jamieson, Fausset-, Brown. Notes on Revelation 2:23.

a)   "Wash" (*pluno*) is "used figuratively of those who by faith so appropriate the results of Christ's expiation [payment for our sin] as to be regarded by God as pure and sinless."

b)   All believers are dressed in white robes (righteousness of Christ). Our "walk" (v.4) speaks of how we conduct our lives, which is the basis of correction here on earth and rewards in heaven (2 Cor. 5:10).

2)   There will be more references to the "book of life," and we will examine its meaning later in our study.

The Church in Philadelphia

The Greek word *Philadelpheia* means "brotherly love." Christ prayed for all believers, in John 17: 20-23, to be brought to complete unity. The Holy Spirit is fully able to prepare the Bride/Church for the return of her Bridegroom, in answer to that prayer.

3:7-8
1)   "The key (*kleis*) of David" is a reference to Christ's lineage through King David, as the promised Messiah. "Since the keeper of the keys has the power to open and to shut, denotes power and authority of various kinds."

2)   To keep His word is to uphold the authority of Scripture, and to live accordingly.

3)   These believers did not deny his name. Jesus alone is LORD.
Read Philippians 2:9-11.

3:9-11
1)   It appears that the seven churches also present a chronological history of the Church from Pentecost to the Rapture. If that is indeed the case, then Philadelphia and Laodicea (vv. 14-18) are indicative of the condition of the end-times Church just before the return of Christ for His Bride (see John 14:10-12 and 17:22-23).

a)   While Philadelphia ("brotherly love") represents the Bride of Christ to be caught up in the Rapture, Laodicea is a picture of the Apostate

Church, which consists of unbelievers within all denominations and independent churches. It will be left behind and continue in its structure, services and members. This view will be developed further in Ch. 17.

b) "Apostasy, 'falling away,' is the act of professed Christians who deliberately reject revealed truth as to:
1) the Deity of Jesus Christ, and
2) redemption through His atoning and redeeming sacrifice... 'Apostates' depart from the faith, but not from the outward profession of Christianity." [10]

2) The true Church will "endure patiently" the apostasy of the end-times by upholding the authority of Scripture and the power of Christ's Name (Rev. 3:8). Therefore, Christ says, "I will keep you from..." From (*ek*) means "out of, from, by, away from."

3) "The hour (*hora*) of trial" is "a definite period of time." This definite period of time is to come upon the whole earth, in relation to His return, which is referred to in the following passage. Read Matthew 24:1-35.

Since Christ is returning for His Bride, which includes every believer (both Jew and Gentile) since Pentecost, and since the prophecies of Revelation Chapters 4-22 describe "a definite period of time" (a time of testing coming upon the whole earth, in conjunction with Christ's second coming), it appears that the Church is being kept out of and away from it. The Rapture of the Church is similar to God's provision for Noah and his family, placed in the ark while God judged the earth with a flood. Read Luke 17:26-27.

When the Church is taken out of the way in the Rapture, it will be sudden and unexpected to the world. Then the "flood" of judgment, the Tribulation period, will come. However, it is the signing of the covenant between the leader of the world empire (Antichrist) and Israel that starts the time clock for the seven years (Dan. 9:24-27).

_____

[10] Scofield, 1304. Notes on 2 Timothy 3:1.

3:12-13

Read Rev. 21:22. If God is the temple and we are the pillars, then we have a secure position "in Christ."

The Church at Laodicea

3:14-16

1) Jesus said, "I know…that you are neither cold nor hot." Jesus knows the true condition of our hearts:

    a) "Cold" (*psuchros*) is "positively icy cold: having never yet been warmed."[11] This is a metaphor of a cold, unbelieving heart.

    b) "Hot" (*zestos*) is "fervor of mind and zeal." The opposite of a cold, unbelieving heart is one fervently trusting in Christ for salvation.

    c) "Lukewarm" is a state between two states (neither hot nor cold): those who claim to know Christ, but do not. We will see this more clearly in vv.17-18.

2) "I wish you were either one or the other." It is easier to lead someone to Christ who does not claim to know Him, than an unsaved "religious" person who claims he does!

3) To "spit you out" (*emeo*) is "to vomit forth." Believers are "in Christ" (John 14:20; Eph. 1:3-14), and will never be rejected. Unsaved church members (those who think they are saved but are not, who have never trusted in Christ as their Savior, but are relying on their own good works to save them) are like food taken in, that your stomach rejects and vomits out. They were never truly "in Christ."

Read John 14:20 (Jesus speaking to his disciples).

3:17

1) "I am rich…" They see material wealth as true riches, making them self-reliant, rather than God-dependent.

---

[11] Jamieson, Fausset, Brown. Notes on Revelation 3:15.

2)   "But you do not realize that you are wretched, pitiful, poor, blind and naked."

    a)   "Poor" (*ptochos*) is "destitute of Christian virtues and eternal riches."

    b)   "Blind" (*tuphlos*) is "mentally blind."

    c)   "Naked" is a metaphor for the unsaved. Believers wear a robe of (imputed) righteousness (Christ's righteousness credited to our account).

    Read Isaiah 61:10 and Romans 4:23-25.

3:18

1)   Christ tells them to ask Him for the kind of gold (wealth) that does not perish even when refined by fire—faith in Him— and He will give it.

Read 1 Peter 1:6-7.

2)   Only Christ can clothe them in righteousness, if they would but ask.

3)   We are washed in the Blood of the Lamb (Rev. 7:14).

"I counsel you" …to get saved!

3:19-20

1)   **There are two views on the interpretation of v. 20:**

    a)   Some see it as a call to believers to restore fellowship with Him (eat with Him).

    b)   Others see it as a call to salvation, since Christ is standing outside. (He's not in the church, and He's not in the heart).

2)   Christ is speaking to the "lukewarm," those church members who profess to be Christians but are not. They are not saved.

3)   Therefore, "Lukewarm Christians" is a contradiction in terms. What most are referring to are believers who are living compromising or worldly lives, what Paul referred to as CARNAL (*sarkikos* = fleshly).

Read I Corinthians 3:1-2.

3:21-22

"To him who overcomes…" Christ offers hope to those with cold unbelieving hearts, and to the lukewarm who make an appearance of faith, to overcome through genuine faith in Him.

Who do you say Jesus Christ is? Are you a true believer in Christ?
Or are you merely an unsaved church member?

If you have never trusted Christ as your personal Savior, asking for His forgiveness, you can pray this prayer of faith right now—and He will receive you as His own:

"Lord Jesus, I believe that You are the only begotten Son of God, that You are fully God and fully human. I believe that You led a sinless life and that You died on the cross for the sins of the world—including mine. I believe that God the Father, by the power of the Holy Spirit, raised You from the dead and that You will come again to judge the living and the dead. I ask you to forgive me and save me so that I can be reconciled with my Heavenly Father, be filled with the Holy Spirit, and live with You forever. I receive You as the Lord of my life and the master of my soul. In Christ's Name, I pray. Amen."

Please refer to the Discussion Questions at the end of the lesson.

Lesson Two
Discussion Questions

Attention Small Group Leaders: Before proceeding to the following questions, please ask the members if there is a topic they want to discuss.

1) What part of today's teaching was unfamiliar to you, and what did you learn today that you did not know before?

2) What part of today's teaching was most important to you, and why?

3) Believers' sins have already been judged on the cross. Instead, we will stand before the judgment (*bema)* seat of Christ at the Rapture of the Church. Jesus will evaluate our lives and we will receive crowns of reward. Please read the notes describing the five crowns (pp. 17-18).

   ❖ How do you relate to each of them based on your life experiences?

   ❖ Which one can we each easily receive, based on no effort of our own?

4) In the message to the church of Laodicea, Jesus is speaking to "lukewarm" members of that church, saying He will spit them out of his mouth.

   ❖ Do you think they are Christians who are living worldly lives, or unsaved church members?

   ❖ Please read the notes for <u>Rev. 3:14-16</u> in your study guide (p. 24). Why is it important to understand the distinction?

27

LESSON THREE: CHAPTERS 4-5-6

♦♦♦♦

The Seven Seals

Overview

We will see in Chapters 4-5-6 that John is given another vision (a continuation of the Revelation), which turns to a scene in the heavens, surrounding God's throne. There he sees 24 elders, and four living creatures who lead the inhabitants of heaven in worship day and night. John sees a scroll with seven seals, but weeps because no one is found worthy to open the seals. That is, until he sees Christ as the Lion of the Tribe of Judah and the Lamb on the throne, slain for the sins of the world. Only Christ is found worthy to break these seals and open the scroll.

The seven seals on the scroll are opened during the seven years of the Tribulation period. The events announced by the opening of the first six seals will occur during the first half of the 7-year period. The first four seals include what we have come to know as the "Four Horsemen of the Apocalypse." Then, the 5th Seal reveals a scene in heaven with the souls of those who will be martyred for their faith during the Tribulation period.

The opening of the 6th Seal begins with a great earthquake, but does not end there. The sun turns black, the moon turns red, and the stars fall to the earth. Every mountain and island will be moved from its place, and earth's inhabitants will cry out to the mountains to fall on them in order to hide them from the coming wrath of God. We will not see the opening of the 7th and final seal until Chapter 8.

Chapter 4: The Throne in Heaven

4:1
1) "After this…" The scene changes from earth to heaven.

2) "…what must take place after this." After what? After the Church Age covered in Chapters 2-3, which will end with the Rapture of the Church. The Church is never again mentioned on earth after Chapters 2-3. From this point on, Revelation speaks of the time of the end: the future 7-year Tribulation period and beyond.

4:2-5
1) "Elders" (*presbuteros*) is "a term of rank or office."

2) What is the identity of the 24 elders?

    a) The elders are dressed in white, wearing crowns of gold. That is a description of Church Age believers from Revelation Chapters 2-3. Do they, therefore, represent the Church?

    b) Or, could the 24 elders be the 12 Patriarchs and the 12 Apostles, representing the Old and New Testament saints? This position seems plausible, but consider the following:

        ❖ Read Rev. 22:12. The Church is rewarded at the Rapture. Jesus' reward is with Him. The rewards are symbolized by crowns.

        ❖ While the souls of the Old Testament saints are present with the Lord in heaven (Eph. 4:8-10), they will not be physically resurrected or rewarded until Christ returns to set up His kingdom on earth (Dan. 12:1-3,13). Therefore, they do not have crowns of reward.

        ❖ All saints will reign with Christ (Rev. 5:10), but only those seated on thrones will have authority to judge.

        Read Rev. 20:4.

❖ Note that those seated on thrones are a group distinct from those who will be beheaded during the Tribulation period.

❖ "throne" (*thronos)* is "a throne seat; hence divine power belonging to Christ; to judges, i.e. tribunal or bench; to elders."

❖ Read 1 Corinthians 6:2. Who will judge the world?

❖ Daniel 7:9-10 *"As I looked, thrones were set in place, and the Ancient of Days took His seat.... (v.10) the court was seated, and the books were opened."* This is the OT prophet, Daniel, speaking of the time of the final world empire and its leader (Daniel 7:7-12), when the Church is in heaven.

❖ In the Old Testament, there were 24 orders of the priesthood. Each order was represented by a single priest. "When these priests met together, even though there were only 24, they represented the whole priesthood...."[12] NT believers are all considered to be members of the priesthood. Read 1 Peter 2:9.

The 24 elders may be described as a tribunal of all Church Age believers, a jury before whom Christ—as the Faithful Witness— will present evidence demanding the coming judgment of the world.

4:6-8

1) The "four living creatures" are cherubim (Ezek. 10:20), angelic beings. They lead the angels and the companies of the redeemed in heaven in the worship of God.

2) They are "covered with eyes" (*ophthalmos*), which speaks "metaphorically, of the faculty of knowing." They reflect the character of God.

---

[12] Walvoord, *Revelation*, 106.

4:9-11

"Crowns" (*stephanos*) are the "rewards of the righteous," not to take pride in but to lay before the throne of God!

Chapter 5: The Scroll and the Lamb

5:1-5

1)   The "Lion of the tribe of Judah" and the "Root of David" are titles for Jesus Christ. He is able to break the seals and open the scroll.

2)   What scroll is this? The prophet Daniel was told to seal up a scroll that concerned "the time of the end," specifically the last three and a half years.

Read Daniel 12:4-7.

This scroll is concerning the final half of the Tribulation period. "A time, times, and half a time" is a 3-1/2 year period that always refers to the second half of the 7-year period, called the Great Tribulation. We will see that the scroll covers the judgments coming out of the 7th Seal, and that the scroll is not opened until the 7th Seal is broken.

3)   "Revelation" (*apokalupsis*) is defined as "a disclosure of that which was previously hidden or unknown."[13]

5:6-10

1)   Jesus Christ is the Lamb of God slain for the sins of the world (I John 2:2). Only He is worthy to open the seven seals (sign of ownership) because He purchased men for God with His own blood.

2)   "He had seven horns and seven eyes…"

a)   "Seven" is symbolic in Scripture of perfection or completion.

b)   "Horn" (*keras*) is a symbol of strength. Therefore, seven horns speak of ALL POWER: God is said to be OMNIPOTENT.

---

[13] C.I. Scofield, 1351. Introductory notes on Revelation.

c) Here again, "eyes" (*ophthalmos*) speak "metaphorically, of the faculty of knowing." Seven eyes speak of ALL KNOWING: God is said to be OMNISCIENT.

d) "…which are the seven Spirits" ("sevenfold Spirit"). This refers to the Holy Spirit (Isaiah 11:2).

5:11-12

"thousands upon thousands" (*murias*) literally, "myriads of myriads; innumerable multitude," and ten thousand times ten thousand. Beyond numbering!

5:13-14

> *Today, you are given the opportunity to participate in this future heavenly scene by putting your faith in Christ as the only means of your salvation.*
>
> *OR... you could possibly live to endure the coming tribulation on earth. We do not know the day or hour.*

Chapter 6: The Opening of the Seals/Four Horsemen of the Apocalypse

The seven seals that are about to be opened are a preview of the entire Tribulation period of seven literal years, as we will learn from a study of the book of Daniel.

We will not see the opening of the scroll until the 7th and final seal is broken in Chapter 8, and it will reveal the coming judgments of God and the events leading up to the Second Coming of Christ: the second half of the Tribulation period, called the Great Tribulation.

With the opening of the seals, it should be understood that the seals are sequential, following in order. However, some chapters in Revelation are an overall picture of some aspect of the Tribulation period. For example, Chapters 17 and 18 are an overview of the judgment of Babylon, symbolic of the world religious, economic, and political system.

Jesus Himself spoke of this time in <u>Matthew 24:3-31</u>. (Please read).

---

*The book of Revelation cannot be understood
apart from the prophecies in the book of Daniel.*

<u>Please keep your place in Revelation, and turn to the book of Daniel.</u>

<u>Read Daniel 9:1-2, 20-23.</u> This passage refers to the time of the Babylonian captivity of the southern kingdom of Israel (Judah).

<u>Read Daniel 9:24.</u> Seventy "sevens" (or "weeks") are 70 weeks of years, or 490 years according to the Jewish calendar. In Hebrew, sevens (*shabuwa*) means "seven, period of seven (days or years), heptad, week." Since the Babylonian captivity was a literal 70 years, years are indicated here.

<u>Read Daniel 9:25.</u> Jerusalem was rebuilt after "seven 'sevens" (49 years). Then, when the additional sixty-two "sevens" (434 years) is completed, "the Anointed One" (Jesus Christ) comes. Jesus Christ presented Himself as the Messiah at what we refer to as Palm Sunday, also referred to as His Triumphal Entry.

<u>Read Daniel 9:26.</u> After the 62 weeks of years "the Anointed One will be cut off," speaking of Jesus' crucifixion. God's program for Israel was interrupted (temporarily) when they rejected Christ as Messiah.

The Church Age is inserted at this point, lasting until the Rapture of the Church, when God's program for Israel will be resumed with what is known as Daniel's 70th week (7 years of the Tribulation). This verse then speaks of "the ruler who will come" as he relates to "the end," a reference to the Antichrist, the final world ruler.

<u>Read Dan. 9:27.</u> The Antichrist will confirm a covenant (peace treaty) with Israel for the final "seven" (years) before "the end," but will break the treaty "in the middle of the 'seven" years. The term "Great Tribulation" refers to the final 3-1/2 years (42 months - Rev. 13:5) of the Antichrist's reign of terror.

Please turn to the "The 70 Weeks of Daniel 9" timeline included at the end of this lesson for your review.[14]

Let's return to Revelation Chapter 6, which begins with the Four Horsemen of the Apocalypse.

6:1-2
First Seal: Rider of the White Horse—the Antichrist

1) The rider on the "white horse" is a picture of the Antichrist, the final world ruler, as a counterfeit of Christ at his return. <u>Read Rev.19:11.</u>

2) He carries a "a bow" with no arrows. The Antichrist appears to come in peace, but is "bent on conquest."

6:3-4
Second Seal: Rider of the Red Horse—War

1) To "take peace from the earth" means "rage and havoc of war."

2) To "slay" (*sphazo*) means to "slaughter, butcher."

6:5-6
Third Seal: Rider of the Black Horse—Famine

"One quart of wheat would be enough for only one person. Three quarts of the less nutritious barley would be barely enough for a small family. Famine had inflated prices to at least ten times their normal level."[15]

6:7-8
Fourth Seal: Rider of the Pale Horse—Death

1) The "pale horse" is "green, yellowish pale."

---

[14] Timeline is by J. Vernon McGee, *Notes & Outlines: Daniel (*Pasadena, CA: Thru the Bible Radio Network) and is based on Sir Robert Anderson, *The Coming Prince: The Last Great Monarch of Christendom* (London, England: Hodder and Stoughton, 1881).

[15] *NIV Study Bible,* 1932. Notes on Revelation 6:6.

2)   For an in-depth study of the meaning of the word "Hades," please refer to the Chart on Hades at the end of Lesson One (p. 13).

3)   How much is "a fourth of the earth"? The current 2019 world population is 7.7 billion people. There are an estimated 2 billion Christians in the world today. If there are 6 billion people remaining after the Rapture, this would mean that 1.5 billion people will die.

6:9-11
Fifth Seal: Souls of the Martyrs Under the Altar

1)   This scene shifts from earth back to heaven, showing the souls of those who will be martyred for their faith during the Tribulation period.

2)   Why are these saints said to be "under the altar"? "In OT ritual, the blood of the slaughtered animal was poured out at the base of the altar."[16]

These are not part of the Church, who will have already been resurrected (given glorified physical bodies and rewarded at the Rapture), but rather are martyrs of the Tribulation period following the Rapture, awaiting their future resurrection (Rev. 20:4).

3)   "Completed" (*pleroo*) means "to consummate a number." God knows the exact number of those to be martyred, and they had not yet reached that number.

6:12-14
Sixth Seal: Cataclysmic Cosmic Event

1)   The "blood" (*haima*) refers to "those things that resemble blood."

2)   To say that the "sky receded" (*apochorizo*) means "to separate, sever." It appears that something will happen to separate the layers of the earth's atmosphere. This is symbolic language describing a cosmic event.

---

[16] Ibid. Notes on Revelation 6:9.

3)   There will be more than one major earthquake (Rev. 16:18-21).

6:15-17

1)   No one will be exempt, either by money or power, from the wrath of God (except by faith in Christ). Read John 3:36.

2)   A natural disaster of catastrophic proportions occurs with the opening of the 6th Seal, which precipitates the time of God's Wrath. In v.17, we see the arrival of the time known as the Great Tribulation.

Please refer to the Discussion Questions at the end of the lesson.

THE 70 WEEKS OF DANIEL 9

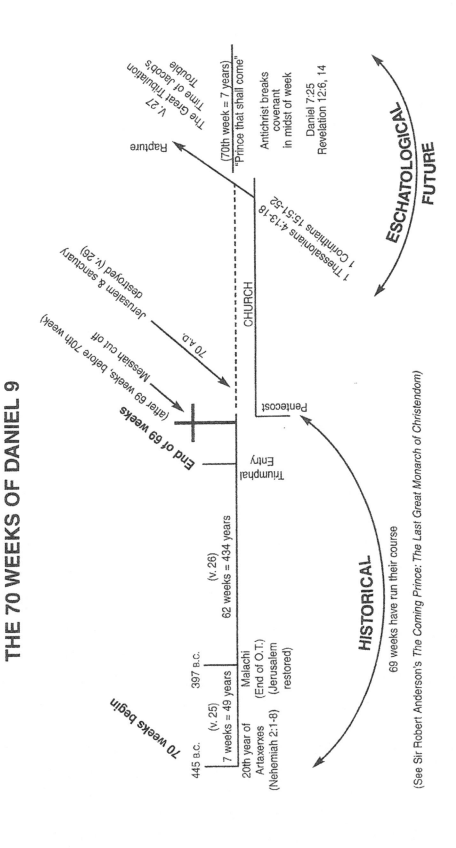

70 weeks begin

445 B.C.
20th year of
Artaxerxes
(Nehemiah 2:1-8)

(V. 25)
7 weeks = 49 years

397 B.C.
Malachi
(End of O.T.)
(Jerusalem
restored)

(V. 26)
62 weeks = 434 years

End of 69 weeks

Triumphal
Entry

(after 69 weeks, before 70th week)
Messiah cut off

Jerusalem & sanctuary
destroyed (v. 26)

70 A.D.

Rapture

HISTORICAL

69 weeks have run their course

(See Sir Robert Anderson's *The Coming Prince: The Last Great Monarch of Christendom*)

Pentecost

CHURCH

V. 27
The Great Tribulation
Time of Jacob's
Trouble

(70th week = 7 years)
"Prince that shall come"

Antichrist breaks
covenant
in midst of week

Daniel 7:25
Revelation 12:6, 14

1 Thessalonians 4:13-18
1 Corinthians 15:51-52

**ESCHATOLOGICAL
FUTURE**

Timeline by J. Vernon McGee, *Notes & Outlines: Daniel, Thru The Bible Radio Network* (Pasadena, CA)

Lesson Three
Discussion Questions

Attention Small Group Leaders: Before proceeding to the following questions, please ask the members if there is a topic they want to discuss.

1) What part of today's teaching was unfamiliar to you, and what did you learn today that you did not know before?

2) What part of today's teaching was most important to you, and why?

3) The identity of the 24 elders is important as we move forward. Please read the notes on Rev. 4:2-5 in your study guide (pp. 29-30), regarding the elders' identity. Do you think their identity as the Church is supported by the points and passages listed? Why or why not?

4) As we step outside of the book of Revelation, into Daniel 9, we see the basis for the belief in a 7-year Tribulation period. Please read the notes regarding Daniel 9 in your study guide (p. 33).

   ❖ Daniel is told of 70 weeks of years (7 x 70 = 490 years) "decreed for [his] people," with 69 of those weeks having been completed at Christ's Triumphal Entry. This leaves one week of years (7 years) yet to be fulfilled. This prophecy relates specifically to the nation of Israel ("your people," v. 24).

   ❖ In Matthew 24, Jesus was asked about the sign of His coming and the end of this age (v. 3). Beginning in v. 15, He referred to this prophecy in Daniel 9, and described it as a time of "great tribulation" (KJV). Who was Jesus speaking to in Matthew 24? (Hint: v. 20 speaks of the Sabbath).

   How does this help support the view that the Church is raptured prior to the Tribulation period?

LESSON FOUR: CHAPTERS 7-8-9

♦♦♦♦

Grace or Judgment?

Overview

In Chapters 7 and 8, we will see that after the Church is "caught up" to be with the Lord (1 Thess. 4:17), God's program for Israel is resumed with Daniel's 70th week, and the task of evangelization is once again theirs. There will be 12,000 "born again" Jews, who have received Christ as their Messiah, from each of the 12 tribes of Israel. A seal of protection will be placed on them before the judgments of God are released upon the earth. These are celibate males whose sole purpose in life is to bring the gospel of the Kingdom to all the world (Matt. 24:14), and there will be "a great multitude" saved during the Tribulation period.

The 7th Seal, and finally the scroll itself, will be opened in Chapter 8 to reveal the judgments of God's wrath, beginning with the seven trumpets.

In Chapter 9, we will see that the sounding of the 5th Trumpet brings a horde of demons out of the Abyss (the bottomless pit, which is the "abode of demons"). They are sent to torment those who do not have the seal of God on their foreheads. A bizarre and terrifying description of these demonic creatures is given. The sounding of the 6th Trumpet releases a literal army from the East numbering 200 million, with a description of modern-day warfare that kills a third of mankind. We are given more insight into this army, their final destination, and the timing of their arrival, from Chapter 16. We are told that the "rest of mankind" did not repent at this time.

Chapter 7: God's Program of Grace During the Tribulation Period

Chapter 7 is an overview of God's end-time program of grace that runs parallel with His program of judgment on earth during the entire 7-year Tribulation period. His "Grace Program" is one of evangelization and salvation, available to all who would believe. The great multitude at the end of this portion of John's vision are the great harvest of souls.

7:1-3
1) A "seal" (*sphragizo*): "Seals were used to mark for each person his own possessions."[17]

    a) All believers are sealed in Holy Spirit. Read 2 Corinthians 1:21-22.

    b) However, this passage speaks of unusual physical protection in addition to spiritual protection, provided for this group of believers.

    c) Other believers will die during the Tribulation period, but will not be affected by all the judgments (Rev. 9).

2) Here, "servant" (*doulos*) speaks of "a slave; metaphor: one who gives himself up to another's will; those whose service is used by Christ in extending and advancing his cause among men."

7:4-8
1) The "tribes (*phule*) of Israel" are explained as "in the NT, all the persons descending from one of the twelve sons of Jacob." (God changed Jacob's name to Israel).

2) These are born-again Jews (following the Rapture of the Church), who have believed in Jesus as their Messiah. Read Rev. 14:1.

3) They are servants of God to spread the gospel of the Kingdom, since the Church has been removed.

---

[17] Matthew Henry, *Commentary on the Whole Bible* (1706). Notes on Revelation 7:2. Public domain.

4)   They will be celibate, unmarried men. <u>Read Rev. 14:4</u>.

      a)   "Defile" (*moluno*) means "pollute, stain, contaminate, defile."
Used here of those Jewish evangelists who will keep "themselves
pure from the defilement of sin, who [will not] soil themselves by
fornication and adultery."

      b)   Here "pure" (*parthenos*) specifically means "a virgin."

5)   While these 144,000 born-again Jewish men are singled out and protected
for service, the Jewish remnant to be saved during this period is not limited
to this group, as we will see in Chapter 12.

7:9-10

1)   "After this..." After what? After the 144,000 are sealed to carry out God's
purposes to spread the Gospel of the Kingdom.

2)   What is the significance of their "white robes"? It symbolizes the imputed
righteousness of Christ, for they have been washed in the blood of the
Lamb.

7:11-15

1)   These are the souls of the multitudes of people from all over the earth who
will come to a saving faith in Jesus Christ before they die in the Tribulation
period. The "great multitude" at the end of this portion of John's vision are
the great harvest of souls.

2)   Chapter 7 appears to be an overview of God's plan of grace during the time
of His Judgment, beginning with 144,000 Jewish evangelists, and ending
with <u>all</u> of the redeemed who will die during the Tribulation period. This
passage does not state that all of these believers will be martyred, as those
described in the 5th Seal (Rev. 6:9-11).

      a)   In light of the natural disasters unleashed upon the earth, many
Tribulation saints will die as a result. With the 6th Seal, one quarter
of the earth's population will be killed (Rev. 6:7-8).

b)   At the same time, it must be pointed out that <u>Rev. 9:4</u> tells us that some judgments (torment) fall only on "those people who did not have the seal of God on their foreheads." All believers are "sealed" in the Holy Spirit (Eph.1:13; 2 Cor. 1:21-22), as belonging to God.

Precedent for their protection from certain judgments is found in the book of Exodus where the Israelites were protected from the plagues sent against Egypt (Ex. 8:22, 9:4, 26, 10:23, 11:5-7).

<u>7:16-17</u>   <u>Conditions these believers will endure during the Tribulation</u>

During the Tribulation, these saints will endure hunger, thirst, burning and scorching heat of the sun, and tears of suffering, but here does not speak of beheading or martyrdom. That will be the case, however, for those who refuse to take the mark of the Antichrist (Rev. 20:4).

<u>Chapter 8: The 7th and Final Seal—The Scroll is Now Open!</u>

<u>8:1-5</u>

1)   The 7th and final seal is broken, and the scroll is now open. It contains the judgments of God's wrath to be carried out during the final 3-1/2 years of the Tribulation period, specifically referred to as the Great Tribulation.

2)   The seven angels mentioned here are not the same as the seven Spirits (sevenfold Spirit) which is the Holy Spirit (Rev. 1:4). These are the seven angels who will be sounding the seven trumpets of judgment.

3)   In the Old Testament, "when the priest entered the Holy Place with the incense, all the people were removed from the temple, and from between the porch and the altar. Profound silence was observed among the congregation who were praying without, and at a signal the priest cast the incense on the fire...."[18]

---

[18] Dr. William Smith, *Smith's Bible Dictionary* (1901). Notes on Revelation 8:1. Public Domain.

8:6-7

We've seen a judgment of hail before, in the Egyptian plague of hail brought by Moses when the Pharaoh refused to let the Hebrews leave Egypt. Read Exodus 9:22-26.

8:8-9

1) This mountain all ablaze may be a volcanic eruption with smoldering lava pouring into the sea.

2) This is literal blood, perhaps from the living creatures that will be killed as a result. In the Egyptian plagues, the Nile was turned to blood (Exodus 7:20).

3) A "third of the ships" implies the area will cover one third of the earth's seas. All of the living creatures and all the ships in that particular area will be destroyed.

8:10-11

1) The Greek word for "star" is *aster*. Scientists have told us that it's not a matter of if, but when the earth will be struck by an asteroid.

2) Here, "bitter" is defined as "contaminated, undrinkable, causing death."

8:12

The earth is partially "turned dark" (*skotizo*) because "of heavenly bodies deprived of light." This was also one of the Egyptians plagues. Read Exodus 10:21-23. Note that the darkness did not extend over the places where the Israelites lived. This may very well be the case for believers during the Tribulation.

8:13

1) "An eagle flying in midair" (*aetos)* is the same phrase used in Rev. 14:6 to describe an angelic messenger.

2) "Midair" (*mesouranema*) is considered "mid-heaven; the highest point in the heavens, which the sun occupies at noon, where what is done can be seen and heard by all."

Chapter 9: 5th & 6th Trumpets

9:1-2

1) Notice the difference between this star and that mentioned in <u>Rev. 8:10-11</u>, which was a literal star (asteroid). "He" of v.2 signifies a personality.

2) What is the identity of the "star that had fallen"? <u>Read Luke 10:17-18.</u> This speaks of the fall of Satan in the angelic rebellion, which occurred prior to the creation of man. We know this because Genesis Chapter 3 tells of the "serpent" (Satan, identified as the "ancient serpent" in Rev. 12:9) tempting Eve. We'll study this event further in Rev. 12.

3) The "Abyss" is "the bottomless pit; the abode of demons."

    a) The fact that Satan is given a key to open it implies that it is locked, a prison for demons. <u>Read Jude 1:6.</u>

    b) Other demons are free to roam the earth, as Satan does, involved in various activities.

    <u>Read Luke 8:26-33; 1 Timothy 4:1; Ephesians 6:12.</u>

9:3-4

1) First, smoke arose from the "abode of demons," signifying their release. Then, "out of the smoke locusts came down upon the earth." As seen in the Egyptian plagues, locusts are a symbol of God's judgment.

<u>Read Exodus 10:3-4.</u>

2) This horde of demons are told not to harm grass, plants or trees (the normal activity of locusts), but only those people who do not have the seal of God on their foreheads.

    a) The 144,000 Jews have the seal of God on their foreheads, but all believers are sealed in the Holy Spirit (Eph. 1:13-14), which is a sign of ownership (purchased by Jesus Christ with His own blood). The protection mentioned here is similar to that which was provided to the Hebrews during the Egyptian plagues. <u>Read Exodus 12:12-13.</u>

b)   Read Rev. 16:2. We see that torment is only for those who bear the mark (seal) of the beast (Antichrist). The mark is a sign of ownership by the Antichrist and, therefore, by Satan himself. Those taking the mark will become demon-possessed (Rev. 9:20).

We know this will take place in the last half of the Tribulation when the Antichrist will reveal his true nature, breaking his treaty with Israel (Dan. 9:27), and the False Prophet will force everyone to take the mark of the beast or be executed (Rev.13:16-18).

9:5-6 In reading Luke 8:26-33, we saw that the demon-possessed man was not free to do as he pleased. Here, because those taking the mark become demon-possessed, they are not free to end their own lives.

9:7-12
1)   Their appearance is not that of normal locusts, but of a completely unnatural creature. John was attempting to describe a creature he had never seen before with language of his day.

Read Joel 1:4. This verse speaks of a literal invasion of locusts, which are symbolic of judgment. Also read Joel 2:1-10, which prophesies a future invasion in the Day of the Lord. In Rev. 9:4-5, these demonic "locusts" are not permitted to harm vegetation or kill mankind but we will see that, with the 6th Trumpet, a literal army will.

2)   Their king is Satan, the angel of the Abyss,[19] called Abaddon in Hebrew and Apollyon in Greek, both meaning "destroyer." He is the thief who has come to kill, steal and destroy (John 10:10).

9:13-16
1)   In Rev. 6:8, we saw that a fourth of mankind will be killed when the "pale horse" is released. Another third would reduce the population by a total of one half. However, many more millions will be killed by the other judgments in addition to these specified.

---

[19] Jamieson, Fausset, Brown. Notes on Revelation 9:11.

2)   The area surrounding the Euphrates River is considered "the cradle of civilization."

    a)   God takes us back to where it all started: Read Genesis 2:2-14.

    b)   Later, the Euphrates was the eastern boundary of the Roman Empire. Today, it runs through modern-day Iraq.

    c)   This ties in with Rev. 16:12-16 (please read).

9:17-19

1)   Not to be confused with the horde of demons sent to torment, this is a real army.

2)   These riders can be viewed as literal soldiers wearing something like breastplates.

3)   The horses are obviously not literal horses, considering the description, but most likely picture future warfare as described by the apostle John:

    a)   their heads resembled heads of lions;

    b)   out of their mouths came fire, smoke and sulfur (symbolic of God's judgment on Sodom & Gomorrah in Gen. 19:24);

    c)   their tails were like snakes, having heads which "inflict injury."

9:20-21

1)   The "rest of mankind" refers to the rest of unredeemed mankind, those who will take the mark of the Antichrist and are past the point of redemption. Read Rev. 14:9-11.

2)   The "magic arts" (*pharmakeia*) spoken of here "signifies the use of medicine, drugs, spells. In 'sorcery,' the use of drugs, whether simple or potent, was generally accompanied by incantations and appeals to occult powers."

Please refer to the Discussion Questions at the end of the lesson.

Lesson Four
Discussion Questions

Attention Small Group Leaders: Before proceeding to the following questions, please ask the members if there is a topic they want to discuss.

1)   What part of today's teaching was unfamiliar to you, and what did you learn today that you did not know before?

2)   What part of today's teaching was most important to you, and why?

3)   Please read the notes for <u>Rev. 7:4-8</u>, regarding the seal placed upon 144,000 Jewish men (pp. 40-41). Some have taken this passage out of context, claiming that this is the total number of people who will enter heaven.

   ❖ Based on what we've studied so far, including the Rapture of the Church covered in Lesson One, why is this not plausible?

   ❖ Where is the group referred to as the "great multitude," which includes all believers who will die during the Tribulation period? <u>Read Rev. 7:9.</u>

4)   What is the difference between the star (*aster*) in <u>Rev. 8:10-11</u> and the star John saw in <u>9:1-2</u>? Please read these passages to discuss. You can also refer to the notes in your study guide (p. 44).

5)   When Christ breaks the 7th Seal and opens the scroll in <u>Rev. 8:1</u>, we see that there are to be Seven Trumpet Judgments. Several of these replicate God's judgment on the Pharaoh of Egypt in Moses' day. List and compare the scope of these judgments.

Overview

As we move into Chapter 10, John sees a mighty angel standing on land and sea, announcing that when the 7th Trumpet is sounded, the mystery of God will be accomplished. John is told to eat the "little book." As the Word of God, it is sweet as honey in his mouth, but the prophecies of judgment turn his stomach bitter.

Chapter 11 opens with the apostle John being told to measure the temple and count the worshipers there. This is noteworthy since it assures us that the Jewish temple will be rebuilt prior to the mid-point of the 7-year Tribulation period. There would not be worshipers in the temple during the Great Tribulation when the Antichrist breaks his covenant with Israel. In Rev. 11:2, we see that John was told not to measure the outer court because the Gentiles will trample Jerusalem for 42 months, which is a reference to the Great Tribulation, the latter half of the 7-year Tribulation period.

The Two Witnesses are the main characters of this chapter, and come at this mid-point of the tribulation, preaching from Jerusalem to the inhabitants of the earth. We know this because when they are killed, we are told that the inhabitants of the earth will celebrate! Not for long, though, because after 3-1/2 days (a day for each year they will preach), they will be resurrected by God and "caught up" in the clouds while their enemies watch. A great earthquake follows the resurrection of the Two Witnesses, and it levels a tenth of the city of Jerusalem.

Then the scene moves to heaven, where the sounding of the 7th Trumpet declares that the kingdom of God has come. The temple of God, which cannot be desecrated, is opened and John sees the heavenly ark of God's covenant.

Chapter 10: God's Kingdom Program—No More Delay!

10:1-4
1) This "mighty angel," as a representative of Christ, reflects His glory and authority.

2) This scroll is not sealed, but only the words of the seven thunders, symbolic of the voice of God. Read Psalm 29:3.

10:5-7
1) The 7th Trumpet is not being sounded at this moment, but in Rev.11:15, which explains the mystery of God to be accomplished.

2) The 7th Trumpet includes all of the remaining judgments through the end of the Great Tribulation.

10:8-11
1) This open scroll is the Word of God. Read Psalm 119:103.

2) While the Word of God is sweet to the taste, the prophecies telling of divine judgments are bitter. We see similar language in Ezekiel 2:9; 3:1-3, which speaks of divine judgment.

3) This appears to be the now-open seven-sealed scroll of judgment in Rev. 5:1. We first saw this scroll in an angelic message given to the prophet Daniel. He was told to seal the words of the scroll until the time of the end. Read Daniel 12:1-10.

Chapter 11: The Temple, The Two Witnesses, and The 7th Trumpet

11:1 The Temple:
"Temple" (naos) is "used of the temple at Jerusalem, but only of the sacred edifice itself, consisting of the Holy place and the Holy of Holies."

The temple is based on the tabernacle in the desert, constructed when Moses led the nation of Israel out of Egypt. It had three sections, including the outer court (Ex. 25-40):

The Holy Place: The place of worship, it contained 3 articles of furniture:

- ❖ The Golden Lampstand (Ex. 25:31-40)
- ❖ The Table of Showbread (Ex. 25:23-30; Lev. 24:5-9)
- ❖ Altar of Incense (Ex. 30:1-10)

The Most Holy Place (Holy of Holies): Separated from The Holy Place by a curtain (Ex. 26:33), it contained the Ark of the Testimony (wooden chest overlaid with gold, Exodus 25:10, 17, 26:34), with two golden cherubim overshadowing the atonement cover (the Mercy Seat), where the high priest sprinkled the blood of the sacrifice (Ex. 37:9). Contained in the Ark of the Testimony:

- ❖ Aaron's rod that budded (Num. 17)
- ❖ Golden pot of manna (Ex. 16:3, 11-15, 31-35)
- ❖ The Ten Commandments (Ex.20)

Note: Here in Rev. 11:1, only the above part of the temple was to be measured.

11:2

1) The outer court of the temple was not to be measured. The Outer Court contained the Brazen Altar and the Laver (Ex. 38). Read Exodus 29:42-43.

"This is where the sin question was settled. The sinner would come to the gate and stand there as a sinner. The priest would lead him into the outer court. The sinner would put his right hand upon the head of the animal he had brought—whether it be lamb, goat or ox. Then the animal was slain and the priest would offer it on the altar. That was as far as the individual went; from then on, he went in the person of his priest. The priest had to stop at the laver and wash so that he could enter the Holy Place."[20]

---

[20] J. Vernon McGee, *Exodus, Volume II* (Pasadena: Thru the Bible, 1979), 297.

2)   The reference to 42 months is the final half of the Tribulation period, which is the Great Tribulation. <u>Luke 21:24</u> tell us: "Jerusalem will be trampled on by the Gentiles until the times of the Gentiles are fulfilled." To trample (*pateo*) is "to desecrate the holy city by devastation and outrage."

3)   The Jewish temple of Jesus' day was destroyed in AD 70 by the Roman army. This passage is speaking of the temple in Jerusalem, which we see here is to be rebuilt. We know this because the Antichrist will desecrate it half-way through his seven-year peace treaty with the Jews (Dan. 9:27).

We're going to step outside of the text of Revelation 11 to gain additional insight.

Let's begin with a review of <u>Daniel 9:24-27</u>.

<u>Read Daniel 9:24.</u>

❖ "seventy 'sevens'" are 490 years in the Jewish calendar

❖ "your people" speaks of Daniel's people, the Hebrews (Jews)

❖ "your holy city" (Jerusalem)

❖ "to finish transgression, put an end to sin, to atone for wickedness"
This was accomplished, for both Jew and Gentile, by Christ on the cross (Isa. 53:6). Since this passage refers to the nation of Israel, it speaks of a future fulfillment during the Tribulation period (Rom. 11:25-27; Zech. 12; Rev. 12).

❖ "to bring in everlasting righteousness"
This speaks of the literal rule and reign of Christ in the kingdom of God (Rev. 11:15).

❖ "to seal up vision and prophecy"
Visions and prophecy will be fulfilled; there will no longer be a need, for God Himself will speak to his people directly (Rev. 21:3).

❖ "to anoint the Most Holy"
This is most likely a reference to the Millennial Temple (Ezek. 40-48).

Read Daniel 9:25.

Daniel is speaking of the first time Jerusalem and the temple were destroyed by the Babylonians, when Daniel was taken into captivity. From the time it was decreed that Jerusalem should be rebuilt, until it was completed, was seven "sevens," or 49 years. Then, it was sixty-two "sevens," or 434 years until the arrival of the Anointed One (Jesus Christ).

Read Daniel 9:26.

After the sixty-nine "sevens" (total 483 years), the Anointed One will be "cut off," speaking of Christ's crucifixion. God's program for Israel stopped (temporarily) when they rejected Christ as their Messiah. At this point, the Church Age is inserted, lasting until the Rapture of the Church, when God's program for Israel will be resumed with what is Daniel's 70th "seven" (seven years of Tribulation).

This verse then speaks of "the people of the ruler who will come, [who] will destroy the city and the sanctuary." Jerusalem and the temple were destroyed again, by Roman soldiers in AD 70. "The ruler who will come," therefore, will be from a revived form of the Roman Empire. We will examine a detailed explanation in Chapter 13.

Read Daniel 9:27.

The Antichrist will confirm a covenant ("alliance, pledge; treaty") with Israel for the final "seven" (years) before the "the end," but will break the treaty "in the middle of the 'seven" years. We know from Daniel 7:19-25, the Antichrist will enter into this covenant as head of the revived Roman Empire, ruled by a coalition of ten leaders (Rev. 17:12-13). It is interesting to note that this global government will "devour the whole earth, trampling it down and crushing it" (Dan. 7:23).

Why would they need to enter into a covenant with Israel? Why not simply "crush and devour it?" Could it be because of the devastating outcome of divine intervention during the Russian/Arab attack on Israel, a prophecy that has not yet been fulfilled, according to Ezekiel Chapters 38 and 39?

The term "Great Tribulation" refers to the final 3-1/2 years of the Antichrist's reign of terror. He will put an end to Jewish sacrifices in the temple and will (through the False Prophet) set up His image to be worshipped. Read 2 Thessalonians 2:3-4; Rev. 13:14-15.

Please turn to the "70 Weeks of Daniel 9"²¹ timeline for review (p. 37).

Let's turn back to our study of Revelation, Chapter 11:
11:3-4

1)   The Two Witnesses in Chapter 11 will prophesy during the final 3-1/2 years (1,260 days) of the 7-year Tribulation (called the Great Tribulation).

2)   The identity of the two witnesses is not stated in Scripture, but we can see the nature of their ministry in vv. 5-6. Jewish law required the testimony of two witnesses for the truth to be established. Sackcloth is symbolic of repentance.

11:5-6

1)   When "fire comes from their mouth," it may be in the same sense as when Elijah called down fire upon King Ahaziah's captain and fifty men. Read 2 Kings 1:10.

2)   "Devours" (*katesthio*) means "by fire, to utterly consume, destroy."

3)   Read Luke 9:28-31. The prophetic ministry of these two witnesses is similar to that of Moses and Elijah, both with Jesus on the mount of transfiguration:

a)   power to prevent rain (Elijah). Read 1 Kings 17:1.

b)   power to turn the waters into blood and to strike the earth with every kind of plague (Moses). Read Exodus 7:20.

---

²¹ Timeline is by J. Vernon McGee, *Notes and Outlines: Daniel* (Pasadena, CA: Thru the Bible Radio Network) and is based on Sir Robert Anderson, *The Coming Prince: The Last Great Monarch of Christendom* (London, England: Hodder and Stoughton, 1881).

Now consider this:

There are two O.T. prophets who did not die: Elijah and Enoch.

1) Joshua 1:1 tells us "After the death of Moses...." which confirms that Moses did indeed experience death. But Enoch, seventh from Adam (Jude 1:14), "walked with God; then he was no more, because God took him away" (Gen. 5:24).

   Read Hebrews 11:5.

2) Elijah was taken up alive into heaven in a whirlwind, as Elisha watched.

   Read 2 Kings 2:11-12.

11:7-10
1) We saw in Rev. 9:11 that Satan was given the key to the Abyss, the "abode of demons," and he rules over them as king. But we will see in Rev. 17:8 that the beast coming out of the Abyss "once was, now is not," ruling out the identity of Satan himself, but rather speaks of an agent of satanic origin, whose identity we will study in Chapter 13.

2) Neither Satan nor his agents can kill the Witnesses until their work is finished. Remember, this happens at the end of the 1,260 days (3-1/2 years) of prophesying in Jerusalem, placing this event at the close of the Great Tribulation, just prior to Christ's return.

3) The great city is Jerusalem ("where also their Lord was crucified"), figuratively called Sodom:

   a) Sodom was a city judged for sin, specifically homosexuality. Read Genesis 19:4-5.

   b) But Sodom is also mentioned in Ezekiel 16:49. (Please read).

   c) Egypt, here, is "metaphorically, Jerusalem, for the Jews persecuting the Christ and his followers, and so to be likened to the Egyptians' treatment of the Jews."

It appears that these will be the characteristics of Jerusalem under the rule of the Antichrist, during the final 3-1/2 years before Christ returns. This will be the environment in which the Two Witnesses will preach, as Jerusalem is trampled by the Gentiles.

4)   Tormented (*bazanizo*) means "to vex with grievous pains of body or mind." It's the same word used for the torment of the demonic creatures in Rev. 9:5 (grievous physical pains); here, of mental torment.

11:11-14
These witnesses will be resurrected and ascend to heaven before their eyes (just as Christ was, as recorded in Acts 1:9).

11:15
1)   Read Rev. 10:7. We see that the "mystery of God" is this: "The kingdom of the world has become the kingdom of our Lord and of his Christ, and he will reign for ever and ever."

2)   The remaining "woe" and 7 Bowls of God's Wrath will occur almost simultaneously: there will be no more delay!

11:16-18
1)   The believer's sins were already judged on the cross, where Christ took our punishment. This passage speaks of judging the "unsaved" dead: The White Throne Judgment. Read Rev. 20:11-15.

2)   The reward of God's servants will occur:
❖ at the Rapture of the Church. Read Rev. 22:12; 2 Corinthians 5:10; 1 Corinthians 3:11-15;

❖ at Christ's return, when the Old Testament Saints will be resurrected (Dan. 12:1-3); as well as the Tribulation Saints (Rev. 20:4-6), both referred to in Rev. 11:18.

11:19
1)   God's temple in heaven, which cannot be desecrated, is opened at the sounding of the final trumpet. Read Hebrews 8:1-5, 9:23-28.

2)   The judgment of an earthquake is sent forth. Because of its timing, it is very likely the worldwide earthquake described in <u>Rev. 16:18-21</u> (the 7th and final "bowl of God's wrath," which will be issued forth from the 7th and final trumpet here in Chapter 11). At that time, the cities of the nations will all collapse, and the mountains will be leveled. This will follow the gathering of the world's armies for the battle of Armageddon (Rev. 16:16).

Please refer to the Discussion Questions at the end of the lesson.

Lesson Five
Discussion Questions

Attention Small Group Leaders: Before proceeding to the following questions, please ask the members if there is a topic they want to discuss.

1) What part of today's teaching was unfamiliar to you, and what did you learn today that you did not know before?

2) What part of today's teaching was most important to you, and why?

3)　　In <u>Revelation 11:1</u>, John is told to measure the temple and count the worshipers there. We know that the Jewish temple was destroyed by the Roman army in AD 70. <u>Please read Daniel 9:27</u>. What does this tells us about the temple in Jerusalem?

4)　　We saw in Revelation Chapters 8-9 that God uses similar judgments during the Tribulation period as those He used in judging Pharaoh in Moses' day. Here, in Chapter 11, the ministry of the two witnesses is similar to Moses (Rev. 11:6), as well as that of Elijah.

❖ Who met with Jesus on the Mount of Transfiguration? <u>Please read Luke 9:28-31)</u>.

❖ Some scholars see the two witnesses as O.T. prophets returning in the end times. Since Scripture does not support the return of the dead, Moses would appear to be disqualified.

❖ <u>Please read Joshua 1:1-2; Genesis 5:24; Hebrews 11:5; and 2 Kings 2:11-12.</u> Discuss which possibilities seem to be most supported by Scripture, if indeed the Witnesses are figures from the O.T.

LESSON SIX: CHAPTER 12

♦♦♦♦

The Woman & The Dragon

Review of Lessons One - Five

I. Lesson One (Chapter 1)

    A) The apostle John is exiled to the Isle of Patmos in AD 95 where he receives a revelation of Jesus Christ in glory and majesty as the Righteous Judge.

    B) Contrast of Two Events:

        1) The Rapture (John 14:1-6; 1 Thess.4:14-18; 1 Cor. 15:51-52) (Believers are "caught up" in the "twinkling of an eye" unseen by the world).

        2) Second Coming of Christ: Rev. 1:7 ("every eye shall see him")

    C) v. 18 Review Chart on Hades (p. 13).

    D) v. 19 Key to interpreting the book of Revelation

II. Lesson Two (Chapters 2-3)

    A) Christ's messages to seven churches are applicable to all believers.

B) The order of these churches reflects the chronological progression of church history moving toward the "hour of trial to come upon the whole world" (Rev. 3:10).

1) Jesus spoke of this as a time of "unequaled distress" (Mt. 24:21).

2) The sixth church, Philadelphia ("brotherly love"), appears to be a picture of the end-times Bride of Christ to be caught up—and kept from—the Tribulation period.

3) The seventh church, Laodicea, as a picture of the end-times Apostate Church (fallen away from biblical Christianity), will co-exist with the true Church, then remain behind after the Rapture of true believers (2 Thess.2:1-4). Here, "rebellion" in the NIV and "apostasy" in the NASB, is *apostasia*, which means "falling away."

❖ "Cold" is a metaphor for unbelievers (having cold, unbelieving hearts).

❖ The opposite of cold is "hot," which represents those fervently trusting Christ as their Savior.

❖ "Lukewarm" is a state between two states. It represents unsaved church members who claim to be Christians but are not saved. They are not trusting in the shed blood of Christ alone to atone for their sins.

III. Lesson Three (Chapters 4-5-6)

A) Chapter 4 is a scene in heaven. The throne of God is surrounded by 24 elders dressed in white and wearing crowns of reward. They represent Church Age believers who will be caught up to heaven at the Rapture.

B) Chapter 5: Christ alone is found worthy to open the scroll with seven seals.

C) Chapter 6:

    1) Review "70 Weeks of Daniel 9" Timeline (p. 37). We know that the Tribulation covers seven years because of Daniel's prophecy in Daniel 9:24-27.

    2) The first six seals are opened in the first half of the Tribulation period. (See the detailed Revelation Timeline at the end of this lesson)

IV. Lesson Four (Chapters 7-8-9)

A) Chapter 7, inserted between the 6th and 7th Seals, is an overview of God's plan of grace and salvation that will run parallel with the judgments in the Tribulation period.

    1) After the Rapture of the Church, the stewardship of the Word of God and Gospel of the Kingdom reverts back to Israel (144,000 born-again Jewish evangelists are sealed for protection).

    2) We see a "great multitude" in heaven, which is the harvest of souls to be saved during the Tribulation period.

B) Chapter 8: The 7th Seal, and finally the scroll itself, are opened to reveal the judgments of God's wrath, beginning with the seven trumpets. The first four are poured out on the earth in this chapter.

    ❖ First Trumpet: A plague of hail causes a third of the vegetation on earth to be burned.

    ❖ Second Trumpet: A blazing mountain is cast into the sea, as in a volcanic eruption, destroying life in a third of the seas.

    ❖ Third Trumpet: An asteroid falls on a third of the rivers and streams, polluting them, and killing many people as a result.

❖ <u>Fourth Trumpet</u>: A third of the light from the sun, moon, and stars is removed.

C)   Chapter 9: Contains the Fifth and Sixth Trumpets.

❖ <u>Fifth Trumpet</u>: Satan is given the key to the Abyss, the abode of demons. A horde of demons is released in the form of bizarre creatures to administer pain, likened to that of a scorpion sting, for five months. This torment is specifically aimed at those who have rejected Christ and taken the mark of the beast (Antichrist). Unbelievers will seek to escape the pain by killing themselves, but will not be able to die.

❖ <u>Sixth Trumpet</u>: Four (fallen) angels bound at the Euphrates River will be released to, in turn, release a real army of 200 million, who will kill one third of the remaining world population, already diminished by previous judgments.

V.   Lesson Five (Chapters 10-11)

A)   Chapter 10: A mighty angel, standing on land and sea, is holding a small open book.

1)   John is told to eat the scroll. As the Word of God, it is sweet as honey, but the bitter judgments it contains will turn his stomach sour.

2)   This little open scroll may be seen as the remaining judgments contained in the now-open scroll of <u>Rev. 5:1,</u> of which John is told to prophesy again.

B)   Chapter 11: The Jewish temple will be rebuilt and sacrifices resumed in the first half of the 7-year Tribulation period.

1)   We are then told that it will be "trampled" by the Gentiles for a period of 42 months, which is a reference to the final half of the 7-year Tribulation period.

2)   We learned from our study of <u>Dan. 9:24-27</u> that the Antichrist will "put an end to sacrifice and offering" in the middle of the seven-year peace treaty, and will "set up an abomination" in the temple.

3)   During this time, two prophets of God ("witnesses") prophesy for 1,260 days, another reference to the final 3-1/2 years of the Tribulation period. No one will be able to harm them or prevent them from preaching until they "have finished their testimony."

4)   After the 1,260 days, the satanically-empowered Antichrist will be able to kill them, but God will bring their dead bodies back to life and they will ascend into heaven as the world watches.

5)   The 7th Trumpet is sounded in heaven, near the end of the Tribulation period, announcing that the kingdom of Christ has come.

Chapter 12: The Woman and The Dragon

Chapter 12 focuses on the nation of Israel, symbolized by a woman described in Genesis 37. During the Great Tribulation, Satan will be cast down to the earth and will pursue the nation of Israel since it is through Israel that the promised Messiah, Jesus Christ, has come.

Satan will work through the Antichrist to attempt to deceive and destroy the remnant of Israel, but God will intervene supernaturally, and deliver them. Aware that he cannot touch Israel, Satan will turn his wrath on the rest of Israel's "offspring," those 144,000 Jewish evangelists and Gentile believers: "all who hold to the testimony of Jesus."

12:1-2

1)   Identity of the woman: We will see from Genesis that this is speaking of the nation of Israel, which will be confirmed in the following verses of Revelation Chapter 12. <u>Read Genesis 37:9-10</u>. Here, Joseph, one of Jacob's (Israel's) twelve sons, tells of his dream.

2) In the Old Testament, the nation of Israel was represented by a woman, the wife of Jehovah God (Isa. 54:5-10), just as in the New Testament the Church is pictured as the Bride of Christ (Eph. 5:22-33).

12:3-4

1) The dragon is Satan. <u>Read Rev. 12:9.</u>

    a) "With [having] seven heads and ten horns, and seven crowns on his seven heads." The "ten horns" are a part of the description of the Fourth World Empire (Rome), from which the Antichrist will come.

    b) We will study the meaning of the ten horns in Chapter 13 and the seven heads will be identified in Chapter 17.

    c) Satan's "tail" swept a third of the stars (fallen angels: <u>Rev.12:7</u>) out of the sky and flung them to the earth." Satan, along with a third of the angels, have already "fallen" in the angelic rebellion, before man was created.

        ❖ <u>Read Ezekiel 28:12-17.</u> "The language goes beyond the King of Tyre to Satan, inspirer and unseen ruler of all such pomp and pride as that of Tyre…. The unfallen state of Satan is here described; his fall is written in Isa. 14."[22]

        ❖ <u>Read Isaiah 14:12-14.</u> Scofield notes: "Verses 12-14 evidently refer to Satan who, as 'prince of this world' system (John 12:31) is the real, though unseen, ruler of the successive world powers: Babylon, Medo-Persia, Greece, Rome, etc. (Ezek.28:2, 12-14)."[23]

2) Satan sought to "devour her child the moment it was born."

    a) <u>Read Genesis 3:15.</u> God is speaking to the serpent (Satan). The woman's offspring" or "seed" is the promised Redeemer of mankind, Jesus Christ.

---

[22] Scofield, 869. Notes on Ezekiel 28:12.
[23] Ibid, 725. Notes on Isaiah 14:12.

b)   This was literally attempted at Christ's birth, when Satan put it in Herod's heart to kill the Christ-child. Read Matthew 2:1-3, 9-16.

12:5-6

1)   This child will rule all the nations with an iron scepter—Jesus Christ!

Read Rev. 19:15-16.

KING OF KINGS AND LORD OF LORDS

2)   1,260 days is 3 ½ years, also 42 months. All such time frames, as they are related to end-time prophecies, are used to point to the Great Tribulation, which begins mid-way through the 7-year Tribulation.

12:7-9

1)   Michael the Archangel is the protector of Israel (Dan. 12:1).

2)   Satan will be forcefully cast down to the earth. "Not the original casting of Satan out of heaven, but his final exclusion—an explanation of his intense hostility against God's people in the last days."[24]

12:10-12

Satan is the "accuser" of the brethren (believers). Satan will have access to God until his final expulsion from the heavens.

Read Job 1:6-11.

12:13-14

1)   We know the male child is Jesus Christ: "who will rule with an iron scepter" (Rev. 12:5; 19:15).

2)   We know that this passage isn't referring to his literal mother, Mary, because it speaks of the time of the Great Tribulation, at the end of world history.

3)   Satan will seek to destroy the end-times remnant of Israel.

---

[24] *NIV Study Bible*, 1938. Notes on Revelation 12:9.

a)   Read Matthew 24:15-25. This is a picture of Israel's escape from the Antichrist when he reveals his true nature in the middle of the 7-year peace treaty.

b)   Read Zechariah 12:10; 13:8-9. This end-times passage tells us that the remnant of Israel will consist of one third of the nation: those who will believe in Jesus Christ as their Messiah.

c)   Read Romans 11:25-27. All (surviving) Israel at that time will be saved believers (Rev. 12:17). They will be taken care of for 3-1/2 years (last half of the Tribulation) out of Satan's reach.

4)   This woman will be given "two wings of an eagle." This is symbolic language of a specific way of escape and a specific place of refuge provided by God, as He did in Egypt at the time of Moses. Read Exodus 19:4.

12:15-17

From Satan's "mouth... spewed water like a river"

1)   Satan will make war against the saints through the Antichrist, described as the "little horn" of Daniel 7. Daniel said, "As I watched, this horn was waging war against the saints..." (Dan. 7:21). We'll study this further in Chapter 13.

2)   "The rest of her offspring" are not the remnant of national Israel, who will be hidden away, but the 144,000 saved Jews who will evangelize the world, along with Gentile believers: all who hold to the testimony of Jesus.

Read Galatians 3:29.

Please refer to the Discussion Questions at the end of this lesson

Revelation Timeline © 2007, 2019 Donna Best

7 Seals of Judgment of the Earth (Rev. 6)
1st Seal: First Horseman (Antichrist)
2nd Seal: Second Horseman (War)
3rd Seal: Third Horseman (Famine)
4th Seal: Fourth Horseman (Death)
5th Seal: Souls of Martyrs Under Altar
6th Seal: Cataclysmic Natural Event

Announcement of Great Tribulation (Rev. 6:17)

The 7th Seal (8:1) covers the final 3-1/2 years of the Great Tribulation including:
  7 Trumpets of Judgment
  7 Bowls of God's Wrath

Battle of Armageddon (Rev. 16:12-16)

Resurrection of O.T. Saints (Dan. 12:1-3)
Resurrection of Tribulation Saints (Rev. 20:4)

Surviving Tribulation Saints enter the Millennium on Earth and continue bearing children (Isa. 65:19-23).

Church Age		Pentecost: Birth of the Church Revelation Chapters 2 & 3 Rapture of the Church		
7-Year Tribulation	**Divine Plan of Grace & Salvation**	First Half of Tribulation: 3-1/2 years	**Revelation Chapters 4-19**	**The Church in Heaven**
		Great Tribulation: 3-1/2 years		
Millennium		Return of Christ with His Bride (Rev. 19:8, 11-14)		
		Satan bound during Thousand Year Reign of Christ on Earth. (Rev. 20: 1-3)		
Satan released to test those born during 1,000 years. Unbelievers rebel and are destroyed. (Rev. 20:7-10)				
White Throne Judgement of the Lost (Rev. 20:11-15)				
Eternity		New Heaven and New Earth (Rev. 21:1) New Jerusalem as satellite City of God above the Earth (Rev. 21:2, 22-27) ETERNAL STATE: All believers having access to the presence of Almighty God! (Rev. 22)		

Lesson Six
Discussion Questions

Attention Small Group Leaders: Before proceeding to the following questions, please ask the members if there is a topic they want to discuss.

1)   What part of today's teaching was unfamiliar to you, and what did you learn today that you did not know before?

2)   What part of today's teaching was most important to you, and why?

3)   How can we be certain that the identity of the "woman" in Chapter 12 is not Mary, the mother of Jesus?

   ❖ We are to look to Scripture for the meaning of symbolism in the book of Revelation. Please read of Joseph's dream, and his father's response, in Genesis 37:9-10. (God changed Jacob's name to Israel). Who does this dream identify as the woman?

   ❖ Please read and discuss the notes on Rev. 12:13-14 in your study guide (pp. 64-65). Who are "the rest of her offspring"? Please read and discuss the notes for Rev. 12:15-17.

4)   In Rev. 12:3-4, we see an "enormous red dragon with seven heads and ten horns and seven crowns on his heads."

   ❖ What is the identity of the dragon according to verse 9?

   ❖ What historical event is alluded to in verse 4?

   ❖ How many of the angels followed Satan in his rebellion against God?

LESSON SEVEN: CHAPTER 13

◆◆◆◆

The Antichrist & False Prophet

Overview

In Chapter 13, we will see the introduction of the revived Roman Empire through which the Antichrist will arise, and another "beast" referred to as the False Prophet. As the representative of the Antichrist, the False Prophet will be given authority over the political and economic systems, and force all the earth's inhabitants to worship the Antichrist or suffer death.

Chapter 13: The Two Beasts

13:1

1) The sea (*thalassa*) is a common reference to the sea of humanity ("chaotic, unorganized humanity").[25] Since Israel is described as the woman in Chapter 12, we see that nations here refer to Gentile nations. The Lord has always set Israel apart from other nations.

2) This beast represents Gentile world empires (to be detailed in Lesson Nine: Chapter 17). However, we will see that the ten horns pertain specifically to the fourth world empire (Rome) spoken of in <u>Daniel 7:23</u>, to be personified by its end-time leader, the Antichrist (v. 5). The word "beast" (*therion*) refers metaphorically (to) "a brutal, bestial man, savage and ferocious."

---

[25] Scofield, 996. Notes on Matthew 4:8.

3) <u>Read Daniel 7:1-8, 17-25.</u> Daniel's vision speaks of four successive Gentile world empires, described as beasts:

<u>First</u>: Babylonian Empire (pictured as a lion, v.4). This is not referring to ancient Babylon mentioned in Genesis 10 and 11, but rather the kingdom of Nebuchadnezzar in Daniel's time (600 B.C.)

<u>Second</u>: Medo-Persian Empire (pictured as a bear, v. 5). Medes and Persians conquered Babylon (Dan. 6:8,12,15)

<u>Third</u>: Grecian Empire (pictured as a leopard, having four heads, v. 6), a reference to Alexander the Great, and his four successors.

<u>Fourth</u>: Roman Empire (pictured as a "terrifying and frightful and very powerful" beast, with iron teeth to crush and devour, "and it had ten horns," vv. 7-8).

    a) The ten horns (Rev. 13:1) are descriptive of the Fourth World Empire of <u>Daniel 7:23-25</u> (Rome), out of which these ten horns (kings) will arise.

    b) These ten horns are ten kings (Dan. 7:23-24), but they are not historical figures of the past. Revelation Chapter 17 places them in the final 7-year Tribulation period.

       <u>Read Rev. 17:12-13.</u>

    c) This tells us that they are a confederacy of kings/leaders living at the time of the Antichrist, briefly receiving joint authority with him.

4) The Lord gave Daniel two visions to describe these four world empires, each with additional insights. <u>Read Daniel 2:31-45</u>.

The statue in four parts:
1) Head of gold (Nebuchadnezzar/Babylonian Empire)
2) Silver chest and arms (Medo-Persia)
3) Bronze belly and thighs (Greece)

4)   Iron legs extending to the feet and ten toes of clay/iron mixture (Roman Empire). This is the additional insight from this vision:

         a)   The Roman Empire continues, in a weaker divided form, until the time of the end. It was never conquered and replaced, as were the previous empires.

         b)   As two legs of iron, the Roman Empire is divided east to west.

         c)   The ten toes on the statue correspond to the ten horns on the fourth beast. The ten toes are ten kings, from both the east and the west. Christ is the "Rock" and His Kingdom will become as a mountain. He will strike the feet, toppling the statue, smashing it to pieces.

The statue of Daniel 2 was in King Nebuchadnezzar's dream, which the prophet Daniel first revealed and then interpreted for him. The four parts of the statue correspond to Daniel's vision of the four beasts in Daniel Chapter 7, signifying the four Gentile World Powers, beginning in Nebuchadnezzar's time and extending until the return of Christ.

The legs of iron correspond with the fourth beast, the Roman Empire. It is important to note that there are two legs, since the Roman Empire was later divided, East and West. The western division of the Roman Empire ruled over Europe, while the eastern division included parts of Asia, the Middle East, and northern Africa, most of which is Muslim today.

The feet and ten toes of the statue extend from the two legs, and correspond to the ten horns of the beast. Both signify the ten kings that we are studying here. Based on what we see in Daniel 7:23-25 and Rev. 17:12-13, these ten kings will rule over a global empire.

That means that there will be ten regional governments, rather than ten nations. The Antichrist will be the leader of the global government who enters into a 7-year peace treaty with Israel at the beginning of the Tribulation period (Daniel 9:27). This corresponds with the release of the first horseman (the Antichrist) in Rev. 6:2, which takes place after the Rapture.

13:2

1) The beast out of the sea has the characteristics of all four beasts (empires) described in Daniel 7:4-8, representing Gentile world power. We will see in Rev. 13:5 that the Antichrist is the mouthpiece of the beast, then becomes synonymous with the beast.

2) The dragon (Satan) will give the beast (Antichrist) his power, throne and authority.

   Read Matthew 4:1, 8-10. The offer that Jesus refused, the Antichrist will accept. Luke 22:3: *"Then Satan entered Judas, called Iscariot."* In the same way, Satan will enter (take possession of) the Antichrist.

3) According to 2 Thessalonians 2:6-8, the Antichrist cannot be revealed until the one who restrains evil is taken out of the way. That is a reference to the Holy Spirit working through the Church.

   After the Rapture of the Church, there will be no restraining of evil, but the Holy Spirit will continue to be at work in bringing people to saving faith in Christ (ex: the great multitude of Chapter 7).

13:3

1) The beast will seem to have had a fatal wound. We will see in vv. 11-14 that the beast coming up out of the earth, the False Prophet, will deceive the inhabitants of the earth on behalf of the Antichrist. (The word "counterfeit" is defined as "to copy or imitate in order to deceive.")[26] The Antichrist is a false messiah. Apparently, he will seek to counterfeit the death and resurrection of Jesus Christ.

   Read 2 Thessalonians 2:3-4, 9-12.

2) "… but the fatal wound had been healed," speaking of both the empire and its future leader (Rev. 13:12-14). Think of the Roman Empire, which appeared to have died, but will be "resurrected" in the last days.

3) What do we know about Satan's ability to resurrect the Antichrist?

---

[26] *Miriam-Webster Dictionary* © 1997 by Miriam-Webster, Incorporated.

a)   We know that "man is destined to die once, and after that to face judgment" (Heb. 9:27). If the Antichrist truly received a fatal wound, his soul would immediately go to Hades ("torment"), and would not be released until the day of judgment (Rev. 20:11-15), when he would be cast into the lake of fire.

Turn to the Chart on Hades on p. 13, and read <u>Luke 16:19-31.</u>

b)   We know that only God can give life. When we read that God will resurrect the Two Witnesses (Rev. 11:11), it was said that "a breath of life from God entered them." Satan cannot resurrect the Antichrist. Satan is, himself, a created being and cannot create or give life to anyone. He can only deceive people into thinking he has!

13:4

1)   "Who can make war against him?" <u>Read Daniel 11:36-39</u>.

2)   Men will worship Satan because he will give his authority to the Antichrist, and they will also worship the Antichrist.

13:5

The beast will be given a mouth— a man, "the ruler who will come" (Daniel 9:26), who becomes synonymous with the beast. We see the beast identified as a man in <u>Rev. 19:20</u>. The beast also represents Gentile World Power, culminating in the Fourth World Empire of Daniel 7, known to be the Roman Empire.

It is often said that the Roman Empire will be "revived" in the last days. It will actually be an extension of the original, even as the feet and toes of the statue in Daniel Chapter 2 extend from the legs, having never been severed (conquered by a subsequent empire). It "seemed to have a fatal head wound" (Rev. 13:3).

13:6-7

He (the Antichrist) will be given political authority over the entire world. This goes beyond the territory of the original Roman Empire, which covered the European and Mediterranean areas.

13:8-10

1)   The names of those who die without saving faith will be blotted out of the Book of Life, which appears to be a register of all those given life from the creation of the world. (This does not refer to children or those not mentally accountable for sin). Some believe Scripture speaks of two separate books: the Book of Life, and the Lamb's Book of Life mentioned here, where a believer's name is written at the moment of their salvation.

     Read Psalm 139:13-16 (at conception); Psalm 9:5; 69:28; Rev. 3:5; 20:15.

     However, those who worship the beast and take his mark will automatically have their names erased from the Book of Life while yet living.

     Read Rev. 14:9-11.

2)   (V.10) *"This calls for patient endurance and faithfulness on the part of the saints."* We will see the same words used in Rev. 14:12. This is in reference to believers who refuse to take the mark of the beast, for which most will be captured and beheaded. Read Rev. 20:4; Jude 1:24.

13:11-12

1)   The False Prophet, like the Antichrist, will be indwelt by Satan (possessed), and used for his purposes. He "spoke like a dragon," like Satan, the Father of lies (John 8:44). Read Rev.16:13, which speaks of his satanic possession, and Rev. 20:10, which tells us of their final destination.

2)   "...like a lamb." Jesus is called the Lamb of God, and He is the Truth. Unlike Christ, the False Prophet is a deceitful religious leader who will force all the earth's inhabitants to worship the Antichrist.

3)   The False Prophet will also exercise authority over the world political and economic systems, on behalf of the Antichrist.

13:13-15

1)   "breath" (pneuma) is "spirit, i.e. vital principle by which the body is animated." Remember that no one can create life except God, and that the False Prophet will use satanic powers to deceive. Read Exodus 7:8-12.

2)   This is "an image (*eikon*), figure, likeness." It is the same word used in 2 Corinthians 4:4 (please read).

13:16-18

1)   The False Prophet, representing the religious world system, will then be in control of the political world system of the Antichrist (v. 12), and as we see here, the economic world system, as well.

2)   While the number seven symbolizes completion or perfection, the number six is the number of man.[27] The number 666 can be seen as Satan's attempt to use mankind to displace God: Satan, the Antichrist, and the False Prophet as opposed to God the Father, Christ His Son, and the Holy Spirit.

Please refer to the Discussion Questions at the end of the lesson.

---

[27] Jamieson, Fausset, Brown. Notes on Revelation 13:16.

Lesson Seven
Discussion Questions

Attention Small Group Leaders: Before proceeding to the following questions, please ask the members if there is a topic they want to discuss.

1) What part of today's teaching was unfamiliar to you, and what did you learn today that you did not know before?

2) What part of today's teaching was most important to you, and why?

3) We saw in <u>Rev. 13:1-2</u> that the first beast (out of the sea) was a composite of the four empires from Daniel's time forward: Babylon, Medo-Persia, Greece, Rome.

  ❖ <u>Read Daniel 2:31-33, 39-43</u> (Nebuchadnezzar's dream of an "enormous dazzling statue" in four parts). Then read of Daniel's dream of four beasts in <u>Daniel 7:7, 23-25.</u>

  ❖ What part of that description points to the Roman (4th) Empire?

4) Based on what we read in <u>Rev. 13:1-8</u>, who is the mouthpiece of the beast?

5) The second beast, coming out of the earth (13:11), had "two horns like a lamb" but "spoke like a dragon."

  ❖ What two identities does this symbolism point to? Who is described as a Lamb in <u>John 1:29</u>? Who is described as a Dragon in <u>Rev. 12:9</u>? What can that tell us about this person?

  ❖ <u>Read Rev. 13:12-14.</u> Why do you think he is referred to as the False Prophet?

LESSON EIGHT: CHAPTERS 14-15-16

♦♦♦♦

The Mark of the Beast & the Wrath of God

Overview

We will see that Chapters 14 through 16 provide a preview of the final judgments of God that will fall upon the earth. John looks down the corridor of time and sees the 144,000 born again Jews, from the 12 tribes of Israel, standing with Jesus on Mount Zion (Jerusalem) after His return to earth to set up His Kingdom. Then, John's attention is drawn to a scene in heaven, where a special group of the redeemed sing a new song. We will see the identity of this group in Chapter 15.

We next learn that three angels will be released from heaven, each carrying a proclamation for the world. The first is a proclamation of the eternal gospel; the second, a proclamation of judgment on Babylon the Great, which we will study in detail in Chapters 17 and 18; and third, a proclamation of judgment on all who worship and take the mark of the beast. Believers are encouraged to endure patiently, since most will be beheaded for not taking the mark of the beast, but "they will rest from their labor, for their deeds will follow them." Chapter 14 closes with the call to harvest the earth, for its deeds are ripe for judgment.

Chapter 15 shows us that the special group of the redeemed we saw before the throne in heaven in Chapter 14 includes those martyred for their faith because they refused to worship the beast or take his mark. Then, the final seven plagues, which are the Bowls of God's Wrath, are poured out upon the earth. Chapter 16, then, is the carrying out of those judgments. This brings us to the battle of Armageddon, just prior to Christ's "Second Coming."

Chapter 14: A Preview of The End of the Great Tribulation

14:1-3

1)   This is the seal of God in Rev.7:3 placed on the 144,000 Jewish evangelists as a physical protection, in contrast to the mark of the beast (which will seal the destruction of all who take it). These Jewish men will live through the 7-year Tribulation, just as the remnant of national Israel will be preserved (Rev.12:6).

2)   "Zion" *(sion)* is "the hill on which the higher and most ancient part of Jerusalem was built; because the temple stood there, it was called the dwelling place of God."

3)   The first scene is that of Christ with the 144,000 on Mount Zion, which is Jerusalem. After this, John heard a sound from heaven, which drew his attention there. The second scene is obviously in heaven because the four living creatures and the elders (Church) are there. Those singing the "new song" are the "harpists."

4)   We saw in Rev. 5:8, that each of the 24 elders, representing the Church, held a harp. These are another group of harpists, not the elders (because they sang before the elders), and not the 144,000.

5)   Read Rev.15:1-3. The harpists are those Tribulation Saints who will lose their lives rather than take the mark of the Beast. Most will receive Jesus Christ as their Lord and Savior through the preaching of the 144,000 Jewish evangelists during the Tribulation period.

14:4-5

1)   The 144,000 will not defile themselves. They will not be "soiled by fornication and adultery." Neither will they commit spiritual adultery (idolatry) by worshiping the beast or taking his mark.

2)   They will be virgins. "Pure" *(parthenos)* denotes "virgin." It is the same Greek word used for the prophecy that the Christ would be virgin-born (Matt. 1:22-23).

3)   The 144,000 may be seen as the first fruits of the saved remnant of Israel.

14:6-7

1) The gospel (*Euaggelion*) is the "proclamation of the grace of God, manifest and pledged in Christ." Read Matthew 24:14.

2) Only those who have not taken the mark of the beast will repent and worship the true God. Read 2 Thessalonians 2:9-12 and Rev. 16:2, 9-11.

14:8

1) Another proclamation: The destruction of Babylon. Is it a literal city or is it symbolic of the world's (pagan) religious system, or is it both? We'll study the symbolism of Babylon in depth in Chapters 17 & 18.

2) To "drink" (*potizo*) the wine of her adulteries, is "metaphorically, to saturate one's mind."

3) The Greek word for "maddening" is *thumos*, and is described as "wine of passion, which either drives the drinker mad or kills him with its strength."

4) "Adulteries" (*porneia*) is defined as "illicit sexual intercourse; metaph. the worship of idols."

14:9-11

1) If anyone takes the mark of the beast, he has sealed his own fate: judgment and condemnation. This refers back to v. 8: he will drink the wine of God's fury because he has drunk the maddening wine of "Babylon's" adulteries.

2) Rather than suffer briefly on this earth, as the believers will do for their faith in Christ, they will suffer torment on earth and in eternity.

14:12-13

Read Rev. 20:4. Most will be beheaded for not taking the mark.

14:14-16

1) Symbolism of the cloud and the reference to "the son of man" most likely signifies Jesus Christ. Read Daniel 7:13-14.

2) A "sickle" (*drepanon*) is "a pruning hook, a hooked vine knife, such as reapers and vine dressers use."

3) To "reap" (*therizo*) means "to reap, harvest; cut off as crops are cut off with a sickle."

4) This harvest refers to people. "Ripe" (*xeraino*) means over-ripe: "to become dry, withered." The same word is used in John 15:6 of those separated from the True Vine, Jesus Christ.

Read John 15:1-6.

14:17-18

1) Here it speaks of the earth's vine, which is opposed to Christ, as the True Vine.

2) Here, the word for "ripe" is *akmazo*, which means "to flourish, come to maturity." Only used here, in Rev. 14:18; it is not the same word used in v.15 (withered). The wicked are ripe for punishment.

14:19-20

1) A winepress (*lenos*) "consisted of two vats or receptacles:

❖ a trough into which the grapes were thrown and where they were trodden upon and bruised;

❖ a trough or vat into which the juice ran from the trough above."[28]

2) Read Joel 3:12-13. "Jehoshaphat" means "Jehovah has judged; symbolic name of a valley near Jerusalem which is the place of ultimate judgment; the deep ravine which separates Jerusalem from the Mount of Olives." Notice the same language used as here, in Rev. 14.

3) "1600 stadia," according to the NASB, is "two hundred miles."[29]

---

[28]Matthew George Easton, *Easton's Bible Dictionary* (1897). Notes on Revelation 14:19. Public Domain.

[29] *New American Standard Bible* ©1995. La Habre, CA: The Lockman Foundation. Scripture quotations from this text are marked "NASB." Used by permission.

Chapter 15: Heavenly Preparation for Final Judgment on Earth

15:1

1) These plagues are actually poured out of the seven Bowls of God's Wrath (16:1). When the 7th Seal is broken, the scroll will finally be opened to reveal the Day of God's Wrath (the second half of the Tribulation, called the Great Tribulation). It begins with the 7 Trumpet Judgments, and here we're told that God's wrath will be completed with these seven last plagues. Read Rev. 6:16-17 and 16:1.

2) These judgments may be referred to here as plagues, since they will duplicate the Egyptian plagues in Exodus.

15:2-4

1) "Victorious" (*nikao*) is used "of Christians who hold fast their faith even unto death against the power of their foes, temptations and persecutions."

2) This passage shows that the harpists in Rev. 14:2-3 are the martyrs who have overcome the beast, by refusing to take his mark.

3) There are two different songs spoken of here:

   (1) the song of Moses (reminiscent of Deut. 32), which speaks of God's deliverance of His people;

   (2) the song of the Lamb.

4) "Beast" (*therion*) is "metaphorically, a brutal, bestial man, savage, ferocious."

   a) "over his image" (*eikon*) is "image, figure, likeness."

   b) The KJV includes the phrase "and over his mark" (*charagma*), which means "a stamp, an imprinted mark, of the mark stamped on the forehead or the right hand as badge of the followers of the Antichrist." This may refer to a tattoo.

15:5-8

1) The tabernacle of the testimony used in O.T. worship was only a replica of this heavenly tabernacle. "The tabernacle of the testimony was the Holy of Holies. Into it none but the High Priest entered, and he only to make intercession for the forgiveness of sins. It is the type of the Holy of Holies above, the mercy seat in the heavens where our High Priest [Jesus Christ] intercedes for us, and where the smoke of the incense of prayer arises to God." [30]

2) "Glory" (*doxa*) is the "majesty of God; His magnificence, excellence, pre-eminence, dignity and grace; God's manifest presence.

Read Exodus 40:34-35 and 1 Kings 8:10-11.

Chapter 16: Completion of God's Wrath

16:1-4

Just as with the Egyptian plague of festering boils, where only Pharaoh and his people were affected, here only on those who take the "mark." Believers will not be affected (Ex. 9:8-9). Water being turned into blood was also one of the Egyptian plagues (Ex. 7:14-18).

16:5-7

1) "I heard the altar respond" is a reference to the souls of the martyred saints under the altar, which we saw when the 5th Seal was broken.

Read Rev. 6:9.

2) "Blood to drink" is a reference back to vv. 3-4. They are given blood to drink because they shed the blood of God's people.

16:8-11

1) Even believers will have to endure these conditions while on earth. Once in heaven, "never again will they hunger; never again will they thirst. The sun will not beat upon them, nor any scorching heat" (Rev. 7:16).

---

[30] Barton Johnson, *People's New Testament* (1891). Notes on Revelation 15:5.

2) As in the Egyptian plague of darkness in <u>Exodus 10:21-23</u> (please read), believers alive during the Great Tribulation may also experience these "pockets of light" or be able to see while unbelievers cannot.

16:12-14

1) A coalition of kings will come from an area East of the Euphrates River. Some view this army from the East as being from the Orient, since the Orient includes all the "countries of eastern Asia," [31] which are also east of the River Euphrates.

    <u>Read Rev. 9:14-16.</u>

2) The four (fallen) angels bound at the River Euphrates will be released for the very hour of the end: Armageddon. We see that the river will dry up, allowing this army to pass over dry land. This army will kill 1/3 of (the remaining population) of mankind.

3) (v.13) Frogs are a symbol of "uncleanness," and are one of the Egyptian plagues (Ex. 8:5).

16:15

Jesus is speaking here of the garments of salvation. Blessed is the believer!

16:16-19

1) "Armageddon is the ancient hill and valley of Megiddo, west of the Jordan in the plain of Jezreel between Samaria and Galilee. It is the appointed place where the armies of the beast and false prophet will be destroyed by Christ's descending to earth in glory, as well as any other forces that will come against the beast."[32]

2) In this context, the "great city" refers back to Jerusalem (Rev. 11:8), as all other cities of the world, including the seat of the Antichrist's government, will collapse.

---

[31] *Merriam-Webster Dictionary.*
[32] Scofield, 1372. Notes on Revelation 19:17.

3) The final judgment on the world has come because God must judge Babylon the Great. Is this occurring because of the sin and wickedness of only one city or only one empire (Rome, as many suppose)? More on Babylon in Chapters 17 & 18!

16:20-21

1) This cataclysmic judgment covers the entire earth. No city or mountain will be left standing, except Jerusalem, which will split into three parts: "…the great city… where also their Lord was crucified" (Rev. 11:8). Jerusalem will survive (Zech.14:10-11), but Babylon, the great city of <u>Rev. 18:10</u>, will be utterly destroyed.

2) <u>Read Luke 21:25-27</u>. The tossing of the seas may be a reference to great tsunamis caused by this world-wide earthquake.

Please refer to the Discussion Questions at the end of the lesson.

Lesson Eight
Discussion Questions

Attention Small Group Leaders: Before proceeding to the following questions, please ask the members if there is a topic they want to discuss.

1)   What part of today's teaching was unfamiliar to you, and what did you learn today that you did not know before?

2)   What part of today's teaching was most important to you, and why?

3)   Proclamations of Three Angels (Revelation 14):

   ❖ Eternal Gospel (v. 6): Do you think this is what Jesus referred to in Matthew 24:14? If not, to what do you think He was referring?

   ❖ The Fall of Babylon: We will study that topic in next week's lesson (Ch. 17).

   ❖ Doom: To anyone who "worships the beast and his image and receives his mark" (vv. 9 – 12). Does this text allow for anyone who takes the mark to later repent?

4)   Chapter 16 covers the Seven Bowls of God's Wrath: "with them, God's wrath is completed (15:1).

   ❖ Following the 4th and 5th Bowls (16:9, 11), we are told that the wicked refused to repent and glorify God. How does this tie into Rev. 14:9-11? Are people able to repent apart from the grace of God?

   ❖ When the 6th Bowl of God's Wrath is poured out, we see that the kings of the earth, and their armies, are gathered at the location of the infamous Battle of Armageddon (Rev. 16:16). How does this passage tie in with Rev. 9:14-16 and 14:19-20?

LESSON NINE: CHAPTER 17

♦♦♦♦

Mystery Babylon

Overview

Chapters 17 and 18 are inserted between the final judgments of Chapter 16 and Christ's return with his saints and angels in Chapter 19. They describe "Babylon the Great," and cover the entire 7-year Tribulation period. This lesson covers Chapter 17 only.

We will go back to the book of Genesis to find the origin of Babylon, so that we may understand the symbolic use of the term in Revelation. We will study other Old Testament passages concerning the worship of the One True God. The comparison will show Babylon as a blasphemous mockery of true religion.

The fall of Babylon was announced in <u>Revelation 14: 8</u>. We will see in this study of Chapter 17 that "Babylon" is symbolic of much more than the idolatrous religious system of the world, but includes the world political and economic systems, as well. In fact, though the destruction of "Religious Babylon" ("the Mother of Prostitutes") has been decreed by God, He will use the political world leaders to carry out its destruction.

This will be at the mid-point of the Tribulation period, just prior to the Antichrist assuming full control (Rev. 17:13, 17; Dan. 7:8, 21-25). At that point, both the Revived Roman Empire and the world religious system will have served their purposes: to bring all the peoples and nations of the world under the control of the Antichrist and his False Prophet.

We learned in Revelation 13, and from our study of the passages in Daniel Chapters 7 and 9, that the Antichrist will reveal his diabolical nature mid-way through the 7-year period of the Tribulation. We also learned from Revelation Chapter 13 that the False Prophet will force all to worship the Antichrist and take his mark in order to buy or sell, and survive. Those who refuse the mark will be beheaded.

A)   In order to understand the symbolic meaning of a word in Scripture, we must go back to the first mention of it and study its literal meaning.

1)   The first mention of Babylon appears in Genesis 10, immediately following the account of the Flood in Noah's time. Read Genesis 10:8-10.

a)   "Babylon" (Hebrew: *Babel or Babylon*) means "confusion (by mixing)." This is significant to our study.

b)   John Walvoord explains:

Ancient accounts indicate that the wife of Nimrod, who founded the ancient city of Babylon, became the head of the so-called Babylonian mysteries, which consisted of secret religious rites developed as part of the worship of idols in Babylon. She was known by the name of Semiramis and was a high priestess of the idol worship.[33]

Note: There is some dispute among biblical scholars as to the identity of Nimrod's wife since she is not mentioned in Scripture. Regardless, we will find that Ancient Babylon is the origin of man's rebellion against God's rule and the beginning of pagan idolatry and practices.

2)   Read Genesis 11:1-9. The beginning of Gentile nations.

a)   Descendants of Noah were told to replenish the earth but were unwilling to separate; they were determined to please them-

---

[33] Walvoord, *Revelation,* 247.

selves, not God. They fell from worship of the true God (the knowledge of which had been passed down from Noah), by establishing pagan religion and human self-rule.

b)   "Babylon" not only represents the confusion caused by mixing false religion with the worship of the one true God, but it was the beginning of, and is therefore symbolic of, Gentile World Power.

B)   The first reference to Babylon the Great in the book of Revelation is in Rev.14:8, "Fallen, Fallen is Babylon the Great, which made all the nations drink the maddening wine of her adulteries."

1)   The Greek word for "adulteries" (or "immorality" used in some translations) is *porneia*, meaning "illicit sexual intercourse; metaph. the worship of idols." Here, also, a metaphor of committing spiritual adultery with a pagan religious system.

2)   Read 2 Thessalonians 2:1-12.

a)   (V.3) "until the rebellion occurs" (NIV), or "except there come the falling away first" (KJV). Both come from the Greek word "*apostasia*," which means "a defection, revolt, apostasy."

b)   "Apostasy (falling away) is the act of professed Christians who deliberately reject revealed truth as to:

(1) the Deity of Jesus Christ, and (2) redemption through His atoning and redeeming sacrifice.... 'Apostates' depart from the faith, but not from the outward profession of Christianity."[34]

c)   Remember that "Babylon" literally means "confusion by mixing." The apostasy of the end-time church will deny the deity of Christ and forsake the doctrine of his atonement (payment for our sins by His blood). We already see this being

---

[34] Scofield, 1304. Notes on 2 Timothy 3:1.

allowed in modern-day seminaries, putting these apostate ministers into the pulpits of our churches, causing confusion about the meaning of true Christianity. This also gives unbelievers a false sense of security. "I'm a good person; I'm going to heaven."

3) <u>Read Rev. 3:14-18</u>. The Church of Laodicea is a picture of Apostasy.

a) "Lukewarm" is a state between two states: neither hot (fervently trusting Christ as Savior, believing that He is God in human form, and that His shed blood is the only means of our salvation), nor cold (unsaved; do not claim to trust Christ).

The "lukewarm" are neither. Though they profess to be Christians, they have never trusted Christ as their Savior; they are not saved. They are merely church members, following an outward form of Christianity, without experiencing a spiritual rebirth.

b) Under no circumstances would true believers be "spit out" (vomited out) of Christ's mouth: Believers are "in Christ" (Eph. 1:3-14).

c) Christ counsels the "lukewarm" to "buy from [Him] gold refined in the fire" which is symbolic of our faith tested by fiery trials (I Pet.1:7). We know one cannot "buy" faith or salvation; this is a reference to <u>Rev. 3:17</u>, which tells us that they were so wealthy they thought they could buy whatever they needed.

d) "White clothes to wear" is a reference to the believer's robe of righteousness (Isa. 61:10), washed in the blood of the Lamb (Rev.7:12).

4) <u>Read 1 Thessalonians 4:16-17</u>.

a)   Those who profess to be Christians but reject the deity of Christ and the redeeming power of His shed blood will not be "caught up" at the Rapture. They are not members of the Bride of Christ.

b)   Left standing after the Rapture will be the organizational structure of the false Church, its buildings, its services, and its members.

This worldwide "apostate church" will become part of the false religious system of the Tribulation period, which had its origin in Ancient Babylon, and has continued throughout human history.

Chapter 17: Mystery Babylon

17:1
1)   A prostitute (*porne*) is "one who yields herself to defilement for the sake of gain; metaphorically, an idolatress." We will see in v.4 that this is a wealthy religious system.

2)   Rev.17:15 explains "many waters": "Then the angel said to me, 'The waters you saw, where the prostitute sits, are peoples, multitudes, nations and languages."

17:2

"Intoxicated" (*methuo*) is a "metaphor of one who has shed blood or murdered profusely." This implies that the idolatry includes the shedding of blood and those who indulge in it will become mentally intoxicated by it (blood lust).

17:3
1)   The "beast" has already been explained in Rev.13:1-2 as representative of the Gentile world empires described in Daniel 7:3-8, specifically the Roman Empire (ten horns) to be personified by its end-times leader, the Antichrist. He will receive his authority from Satan himself (Rev. 13:4-5).

2) This is one beast with seven heads, explained in vv.9-10: *"They are seven hills on which the woman sits. They are also seven kings."* (*Hills* translated as *mountains* (*oros*) in NASB). *"*Mountains' have a symbolical meaning, namely, prominent seats of power."[35] Therefore, we can say that the heads represent both the kings and their kingdoms.

3) The ten horns are explained in v.12, *"The ten horns you saw are ten kings who have not yet received a kingdom but who for one hour will receive authority as kings along with the beast."*

    a) This tells us that they are a confederacy of kings/leaders living at the time of the Antichrist, briefly receiving joint authority with him.

    b) These ten horns are descriptive of the Fourth World Empire (Roman Empire) of Daniel 7:23-25, out of which these ten horns (kings) will arise. The Roman Empire, which no longer exists in its original form, will have to be restored.

Note: You may want to read Daniel 2 to review the meaning of the statue. The legs of iron are symbolic of the Roman Empire. They are not "cut off" (conquered by a later empire) but rather extend to the feet and ten toes.

17:4-5
1) "Abomination" *(bdelugma)* refers to "a foul thing, a detestable thing; of idols and things pertaining to idolatry." Read Exodus 20:1-4.

2) Mystery Babylon is dressed lavishly, signifying great wealth.

3) "Mystery" (*musterion*) is a "hidden thing… generally religious secrets." This woman is a religious symbol.

4) "Mother" (*meter*) is a "metaphor, the source of something."

5) The ancient city of Babylon was the source of idolatrous religion ("Mother of Prostitutes"). "Religious Babylon," the religious system of the Revived Roman Empire, is one woman riding the beast, symbolic of a one-world

---

[35] Jamieson, Fausset, Brown. Notes on Revelation 17:9.

religion, a fusion of religions which "yield themselves to defilement for the sake of gain" (*porne*).

17:6-7

1) The phrase "drunk with blood" is the same as "intoxicated" in v.2 (*methuo*), which is a "metaphor of one who has shed blood or murdered profusely." This is blood lust: this religious system will persecute and kill in the name of religion. The Fifth Seal Judgment (Rev. 6:9-10) tells us that many believers will be slain during the first half of the Tribulation, "because of the Word of God and the testimony they maintained."

2) "The mystery of the woman and the beast she rides…" Let's wait to read the angel's explanation.

17:8

1) The explanation of this beast is found in vv. 9-11.

The Abyss (*Abussos*) is the "abode of demons." Satan is their king (Rev. 9:11), since demons are fallen angels who followed him in his rebellion against God. This speaks of its satanic origin.

2) Book of Life: register of all who have been given life. Read Psalm 139:16.

17:9-11

1) "This calls for a mind with wisdom." Read James 1:5.

2) The heads on the beast were not included in Daniel's description of the original Roman Empire, but only a reference to the ten horns. He described four World Empires: Babylon (not the ancient city from Genesis 10, 11. The vision refers to the Babylonian empire of Daniel's day), Medo-Persia, Greece, and Rome.

Read Daniel 7 (entire chapter).

Prior to Daniel's time there were, however, two historically recognized great empires, Egypt and Assyria, both mentioned in the Old Testament for taking God's people into captivity. Read Exodus 1:1-14; 2 Kings 17:21-23.

3) These seven heads are successive kings/kingdoms, not the confederacy of kings/ kingdoms listed as "ten horns."

    a) <u>Five have fallen</u>: Egypt, Assyria, Babylon, Medo-Persia, Greece.

    b) <u>One is</u>: Rome (in John's day).

    c) <u>The other has not yet come,</u> but when it does come, he/it must remain for a little while: the Revived Roman Empire, personified by its leader, the Antichrist. <u>Read Rev. 13:3</u>.

    d) The original Roman Empire did not extend over the entire earth, but over the European and Mediterranean areas. The revived Roman Empire, the seventh kingdom, will "devour the whole earth" (Daniel 7:23, Rev. 13:7-8).

       The Antichrist (the "little horn" of Daniel 7) will join with the ten horns "for a little while," then the ten kings will "give their power and authority to the beast" (Antichrist - Rev.17:13).

4) We saw that this beast (Gentile World Power) originated in Ancient Babylon (Genesis 10-11), which once was, now is not (in John's day), and becomes the 8th kingdom. The king and his kingdom are synonymous. Both are going to their destruction (Rev. 18:10; 19:20).

    The Antichrist is, therefore, the 8th king of the 8th kingdom, called Babylon here in Revelation Chapters 17 and 18 because of its roots in Ancient Babylon (Genesis 10-11), all having a satanic origin ("coming up out of the Abyss").

5) The "prostitute," Religious Babylon (false religious system), sits on and is carried on the back of ALL the Gentile World powers (political Babylon), from the beginning (Genesis 11) through the end of world history.

17:12-14

1) A future kingdom, not in John's day. This speaks of the Revived Roman Empire that "must remain for a little while."

2) The "beast" is here personified in the Antichrist. The ten kings' positions are short-lived. They have only one purpose: to give their authority over to the Antichrist. Then the Antichrist will reign as final world dictator for the last 3-1/2 years of the Tribulation period (called the Great Tribulation).

3) Drawn to the battle of Armageddon (Rev.16:16), the kings of the earth will make war against the Lamb, when Christ returns with "the armies of heaven" (Rev.19:14).

17:15-17

1) "Sits" (*kathemai*) is "to have a fixed abode; to dwell." This idolatrous worship system has had "a fixed abode" among the peoples and nations of the earth.

2) Here, we see that the religious world system, personified by this prostitute, rides on the back of the political world system.

    a) In <u>Rev. 17:7</u>, the NIV states: "the beast she rides." The NASB translates it as "the beast that carries her." "Carries" (*bastazo*) means "to bear what is burdensome."

    b) The one who sits on the beast leads and controls it. Up to this point, the government will be controlled by this religious system, as we see in Islamic states such as Iran. It will be "burdensome." For this reason, the empire will seek to destroy the one-world religious system since she has served her purpose in uniting the nations. They now want to be free of her control.

3) To "bring her to ruin" (*eremoo*) is "to despoil one; strip her of her treasures."

4) To "eat her flesh" (*esthio*) is "to devour, to consume." We are not told exactly how. This happens prior to Chapter 18, where the final destruction of the entire world system is complete.

5) (v.17) God is COMPLETELY in control of the outcome.

<u>Read Proverbs 21:1</u>.

17:18

1)   "The woman" is the Mother (*meter* = source) of Prostitutes (v.5).

2)   The term "Babylon" is a symbolic term, a reference to the ancient city of Babylon, which was the source of idolatrous worship and Gentile world power. A literal city has not "ridden on the back" of all the empires since Ancient Babylon (Genesis 10-11).

      However, it is not difficult to understand that the final world empire requires a seat of government: a city that will be destroyed along with the system. Here, Babylon may be taken literally: the ancient city of Babylon, located in modern-day Iraq, may yet be rebuilt.

3)   "Babylon" is, therefore, a satanic system (Rev. 12:3):

      a)   Religious Babylon: the source of idolatrous worship ("Mother of Prostitutes," Rev. 17:5)

      b)   Political Babylon: Gentile World Power, with the final world empire controlled by the Antichrist (Rev. 13:5-9).

      c)   Economic Babylon: the World economic system, finally controlled by the False Prophet. The mark of the beast and worship of his image are required in order to buy or sell (Rev. 13:15-17).

Please refer to the Discussion Questions at the end of the lesson.

Lesson Nine
Discussion Questions

Attention Small Group Leaders: Before proceeding to the following questions, please ask the members if there is a topic they want to discuss.

1) What part of today's teaching was unfamiliar to you, and what did you learn today that you did not know before?

2) What part of today's teaching was most important to you, and why?

3) Based on Rev. 17:6-7, who is it that will kill many believers during the first half of the Tribulation period? Who will seek to kill them during the second half (Dan. 7:23-25)?

4) In Rev. 17:9-11, the seven heads of the beast are seven biblical and historical kingdoms or empires. We know this because this same beast (as described in Rev. 13:1-2) is a composite of the four beasts of Daniel 7, which are four kingdoms from Daniel's time forward (Dan. 7:16-25).

   ❖ We also know there were two prominent kingdoms prior to Daniel's time (known for taking the Israelites into captivity), and one yet to come. Name the six kingdoms. What is the 7th kingdom?

   ❖ What is the 8th kingdom and who is its king?

   ❖ Please review and discuss your answers based on the notes in your study guide on Rev. 17:9-11 (pp. 91-92).

LESSON TEN: CHAPTER 18

◆◆◆◆

The Destruction of Babylon

Review of Chapter 17

Revelation Chapters 17 and 18 have to do with the overall theme of Babylon in the 7-year Tribulation period. Let's review the key figures and names in Chapter 17 before moving on to this week's lesson.

We saw a woman who, we are told, sat on many waters. "Many waters" was explained in Rev. 17:15 as symbolic of "peoples, multitudes, nations, and languages," a reference to all the earth. She was also seen riding on a beast, and the beast had seven heads and ten horns (Rev. 17:3). The woman was described as "a great prostitute" with a title written on her forehead: "Mystery, Babylon the Great, the Mother of Prostitutes and of the Abominations of the earth." "Abominations" (*bdelugma*) speak of "idols and things pertaining to idolatry."

In order to understand the symbolic meaning of Babylon, we went back to the first mention of it in the book of Genesis, Chapters 10 and 11. There we found that Ancient Babylon was the "mother" or "source" of both pagan idolatry and human self-government, both of which oppose the worship of, and submission to, the one true God.

The woman relates to a pagan religious system. We saw that the "beast she rides" is a reference to human government, which we can refer to as Gentile World Power. This is one woman riding one beast, indicating an end-time religious system riding upon a global government.

In Lesson Seven, we gleaned information from Daniel's interpretation of Nebuchadnezzar's dream in Daniel 2, and of his vision of the four beasts in Daniel 7. Both referred to four world powers from Daniel's time forward, which were Babylon (not Ancient Babylon, but the one ruled by Nebuchadnezzar in Daniel's day), Medo-Persia, Greece, then Rome. Each of the first three empires was defeated by the next, but the Roman Empire was not defeated. It merely extended through to the end-times in a weakened form (the feet of iron mixed with clay in the statue of Daniel 2).

From Daniel 7, we learned that the fourth kingdom (Rome) would eventually crush and devour the whole earth (v.23). The ten horns on one of the seven heads on this beast were explained to be ten kings who would come from this kingdom, forming what would be a 10-region global government. Dan.7:24 tells us that after they have formed a confederacy, "another king will arise" and take leadership. This king is known as the Antichrist, for he claims to be God (2 Thess. 2:4).

Then, we received additional insight about the ten-king confederacy in Revelation 13 and 17. Revelation 17:12 tells us that they will rule with the Antichrist for a brief period of time: the first 3-1/2 years of the Tribulation period and possibly some time before that, since the global government will have to be in place prior to the Antichrist making a 7-year peace treaty with Israel (Dan. 9:27).

Revelation 17:13 tells us that these ten kings/leaders "have one purpose and will give their power and authority to the beast" (Antichrist). Daniel 7:25 tells us it will be for "a time, times, and half a time," which is a reference to the final 3-1/2 years of the tribulation period during which the Antichrist will reign. This final kingdom under the total control of the Antichrist is also called Babylon in Chapter 18, and is satanic in origin.

He will grant authority to the person called the "False Prophet," who will order "them to set up an image in honor of the Antichrist so that it will speak and cause all who refuse to worship the image to be killed."

He will also force everyone "to receive a mark on his right hand or on his fore-head, so that no could buy or sell unless he had the mark" (Rev. 13:14-17).

READ ALL OF REVELATION 17

Seven Kingdoms (17: 9-11): (*Hills* translated as *mountains* (*oros*) in NASB). "Mountains' have a symbolical meaning, namely, prominent seats of power."[36] Therefore, we can say that the heads represent both the kings and their kingdoms.

1) The heads on the beast were not included in Daniel's description of the original Roman Empire, but only a reference to the ten horns. He described four World Empires from his lifetime forward:

    Babylon (not ancient city from Genesis 10. The vision refers to Babylonian empire of Daniel's day), Medo-Persia, Greece, and Rome.

2) Prior to Daniel's time there were, however, two historically recognized great empires, Egypt and Assyria, both mentioned in the Old Testament for taking God's people into captivity. Read Ex. 1:1-14 and 2 Kings 17:21-23.

3) These seven heads are successive kings/kingdoms, not the end-time confederacy of kings/kingdoms listed as the "ten horns."

    a) Five have fallen: Egypt, Assyria, Babylon, Medo-Persia, Greece.

    b) One is: Rome (in John's day).

    c) The other has not yet come, but when it does come, he/it must remain for a little while: Revived Roman Empire, personified by its leader, the Antichrist. Read Rev. 13:3.

    d) The original Roman Empire did not extend over the entire earth, but over the European and Mediterranean areas. The revived Roman Empire, the seventh kingdom, will "devour the whole earth" (Daniel 7:23, Rev. 13:7-8).

        The Antichrist (the "little horn" of Daniel 7) will join with the ten horns "for a little while," then the ten kings will "give their power and authority to the beast" (Antichrist - Rev.17:13).

---

[36] Jamieson, Fausset, Brown. Notes on Revelation 17:9.

4) We saw that this beast (Gentile World Power) originated in Ancient Babylon (Genesis 10-11), "which once was, now is not" (in John's day), and becomes the 8th kingdom. The king and his kingdom are synonymous. Both are going to their destruction (Rev. 18:10; 19:20).

The Antichrist is, therefore, the 8th king of the 8th kingdom, called Babylon here in Revelation Chapters 17-18 because of its roots in Ancient Babylon (Genesis 10-11), all having a satanic origin ("coming up out of the Abyss").

5) The "prostitute," Religious Babylon (false religious system), sits on and is carried on the back of ALL the Gentile World powers (political Babylon), from the beginning through the end of world history.

Overview of Chapter 18:

In order to understand the prophecies concerning Babylon that are contained in Chapters 17-18, we must see it in its entirety: a satanic world system that began in Ancient Babylon, and encompasses false religion and human self-rule in the political and economic realm of the Gentile World Empires.

The first stage of the destruction of Babylon, presented in Chapter 17, was the dismantling of the religious system, which God will bring about by using the kings or leaders of the Revived Roman Empire (Rev. 17:17). Here, in Chapter 18, we will see the judgments of God brought to bear on the economic and political segments of the final world empire, and on the great city that is the seat of its government. The destruction of all human self-government will be complete and will never "be found again" (Rev. 18:21).

18:1

To "illuminate" (*photizo*) is "to give light; to shine." The brightness of this angel's splendor is produced by the authority he is given by God.

1) All authority comes from Christ (Matt. 28:18). As we walk in His authority, we reflect God's glory.

2)   The glory of God (His manifest Presence) is revealed in us when the Kingdom of God RULES in us. A servant of God is one who is fully surrendered to God for the advancement of His Kingdom on earth, which must begin as His Kingdom authority rules in our own hearts and lives. Therefore, we must pray for His will to be done and His Kingdom to come *in us*, then *through us*, to the world around us, that He may be glorified.

18:2-3

1)   This is again a reference to the "Mother of Prostitutes" (17:5), specifically the world religious system "birthed" in Ancient Babylon, which will be brought "to ruin" by the kings of the earth (17:16). Remember that the "Prostitute" (religious Babylon) rode on the backs of the world empires, and was a burden to them.

2)   However, the reference to Babylon is two-fold: the religious system and the political/economic system. The religious system is said to be destroyed in one day (v.8), while the political/economic system will be destroyed in one hour (v. 19).

3)   "The kings of the earth" is a reference to the political aspect of the system. It will commit spiritual "adultery" (idolatry) with the religious system.

4)   The "Abyss" will be the dwelling place of demons until they are released (Chapter 9). Then the earth will become "a home for demons." Imagine it!

18:4-6

1)   To "share in" (*sugkoinoneo*) is "to become a partaker together with others, or to have fellowship with a thing." This is the same word used in Ephesians 5:11 (please read).

2)   Read 1 John 2:15-17. Instead, we are to "participate in the divine nature and escape the corruption in the world caused by evil desires" (2 Pet. 1:4).

18:7-8

1)   To give oneself "luxury" (*streniao*) is "to be wanton (sensuous), to live luxuriously." Read James 5:1-6.

2) Up to this point, Chapter 18 appears to refer back to the religious system, which will be destroyed by the ten kings (Rev. 17:16).

However, "Babylon" is also a city: the seat of the world empire (Rev. 17:18).

18:9-10

1) The kings of the earth will hate and destroy "Religious Babylon" (Rev. 17:15-18). Here, they mourn over the collapse of the economic system and disintegration of the empire, symbolized by the "city of power."

2) Babylon is symbolic of both the religious system (Mother of Prostitutes) and Gentile World Power. "The woman you saw is [also] the great city that rules over the kings of the earth" (Rev. 17:18)

3) "Power" (*ischuros*), as used here, is "strong, firm, sure." The unsaved of the world will believe this city/system to be indestructible.

4) The religious system will be destroyed in one day (Rev. 18:8). Here, the political/economic system will be destroyed in one hour.

18:11-13

1) The "merchants of the earth" represent commerce, i.e. the economy.

2) The "bodies and souls of men" speaks of human trafficking, already taking place, especially in using children for sex trade and pornography.

18:14-16

1) "The fruit the world longed for" (lusted after) is in stark contrast to the "fruit of the Spirit." Read Galatians 5:22-23.

2) "All your riches…" (NIV), referred to as "all things that were luxurious and splendid" in the NASB.

3) "Luxurious" (*liparos*) refers to "things which pertain to a sumptuous and delicate style of living."

4)   "Splendid (*lampros*) things, i.e. luxuries or elegancies in dress or style."

18:17-18

This "great city," as the seat of the final world empire, is symbolic of Gentile World Power from the beginning. This city will be the most spectacular of all.

18:19-20

1)   God's judgment is upon the entire world system, not on a city or a particular empire (ex: Rome), or its false religion. Here, specifically, it is concerning the way the world has persecuted the saints of God. Read Rev. 6:9-11.

Read Rev. 12:17. The dragon is Satan (12:9); the woman here is the nation of Israel, and those who hold to the testimony of Jesus are Jewish and Gentile believers, all "Abraham's seed" (Gal. 3:29). This speaks of the satanic origin of this persecution.

2)   However, Satan will use the Antichrist and his political power to bring this about: "He (Antichrist) was given power to make war against the saints and to conquer them" (Rev. 13:7). This speaks of persecution of the saints (Christians) by world governments.

3)   Read Rev. 17:6. The woman here is Babylon: Mother of Prostitutes. This speaks of the persecution of the saints by false religions.

18:21-23

After the destruction of the world religious system (Ch.17), the False Prophet is given the authority of the Antichrist to force the earth's inhabitants to worship the image of Antichrist and take his mark, in order to buy or sell. He "leads the nations astray" through sorcery!

Read Rev. 13:13-17.

18:24

1)   "The blood of prophets and of the saints" is not found in one literal city. Again, this speaks of the entire satanic world system, for Satan is the "god of this world" (2 Cor. 4:4).

2) "The blood of all who have been killed on earth" speaks not only of the saints, but of all the bloodshed throughout history.

Please refer to the Discussion Questions at the end of the lesson.

Lesson Ten
Discussion Questions

Attention Small Group Leaders: Before proceeding to the following questions, please ask the members if there is a topic they want to discuss.

1)   What part of today's teaching was unfamiliar to you, and what did you learn today that you did not know before?

2)   What part of today's teaching was most important to you, and why?

3)   We learned in <u>Rev. 17:18</u> that Babylon (symbolic of the world religious system) is also "the great city that rules over the kings of the earth." That city is the seat of, and therefore, representative of the final world government ruled by the Antichrist.

   ❖ If the symbolism of Babylon extends beyond the religious system to the kingdom of the Antichrist (the 8th king of the 8th kingdom—Rev. 17:11), who/what is represented by the beast she rides (17:3)?

   ❖ After discussing, please review your study guide notes for <u>Rev. 17:18</u> (p. 94).

4)   <u>Rev. 18:1-8</u> appears to refer back to the one-world religious system known as Babylon, the Mother of Prostitutes, in Chapter 17. Let's look at some contrasts between the destruction of the religious system, and that of the Antichrist's final government.

   ❖ In <u>Rev. 17:16</u>, we learned that the ten kings (of the Revived Roman Empire) will hate and destroy the prostitute. Compare their reaction in <u>17:16 </u>to their reaction to the destruction of the seat of the Antichrist's kingdom in <u>Rev. 18:15-19</u>.

   ❖ Discuss the timeline of each. At what point in the Tribulation will the one-world religious system be destroyed? (Read Rev. 17:17). When will the Antichrist's government be destroyed? After discussing, please read <u>Rev. 16:16-19</u> and your study guide notes on that passage (pp. 82-83).

LESSON ELEVEN: CHAPTERS 19-20

♦♦♦♦

Christ Returns for His Thousand-Year Reign

Overview

Chapter 19 is full of rejoicing in heaven, since the satanic world system of Babylon is finally judged for its wickedness and for shedding the blood of the saints. God is praised, and the Church as the Bride of Christ is prepared for the wedding supper of the Lamb, Jesus Christ. The scene transitions to earth, as Christ returns with His Bride and His holy angels.

We can also anticipate that included in this great army are the souls of the Old Testament and Tribulation saints, who will be physically resurrected on earth (Dan. 12:1-3; Rev. 20:4-6). We saw this pattern established at the Rapture, when the souls of deceased church age believers returned with Christ to be physically resurrected (I Thess. 4:14-17).

At His Second Coming, Christ will not be a suffering servant. He will come as the Righteous Judge who slays the wicked and no longer tolerates sin or rebellion against His authority. The Antichrist and the False Prophet will be no match for Him, and they will be thrown alive into the lake of burning sulfur (hell). Satan will be bound in the Abyss (the "abode of demons") for a thousand years.

No unsaved person will enter Christ's thousand-year reign on earth. In keeping with God's plan that man freely choose Christ as Savior, we will see that at the end of the thousand years, Satan will be released to test those born during the Millennium. There will be a final battle where all those in rebellion will perish.

If you recall from our study in Lesson One, the souls of the unsaved are held in Hades until that time when the unsaved from all ages will be physically resurrected to face the White Throne Judgment of God. Chapter 20 ends with the judgment of the wicked, whose names were not found in the Book of Life, being thrown (body and soul) into the lake of fire.

Chapter 19: Christ Returns to the Earth with His Bride

Chapters 17 and 18 were an overview of the pagan religious system and human self-rule that had been "birthed" in Ancient Babylon. As for the sequence of events, however, Chapter 19 chronologically follows Chapter 16 and coincides with the end of Chapter 18.

19:1-3

1)   After the destruction of "Babylon," the satanic world religious, economic, and political system, John heard the great multitude in heaven shouting. The timing coincides with what we've seen in Chapter 16.

        Read Rev. 16:12-21.

2)   The "great multitude" was first seen in Chapter 7, identified as "they who have come out of the great tribulation." They are seen as a group distinct from the Lamb and His Bride.

19:4-8

1)   The Church, previously represented by the 24 elders, makes herself ready as the Bride. The judgment seat of Christ and the rewarding of Church saints will follow the Rapture (Rev. 22:12). This will already have taken place before the Tribulation period begins, as shown by the 24 elders seated on thrones (Rev. 4:4), and laying their crowns of reward before the throne of God in Rev. 4:10.

2)   Here, the Church is corporately provided with a glorious gown, made from the righteous acts of the saints, in preparation for the wedding. These righteous acts were prepared in advance by God, and done through the power of the Holy Spirit, so that it is God's work from beginning to end, and God gets the glory!! Read Ephesians 2:10.

3) This appears to place the timing of the wedding supper of the Lamb after the Great Tribulation on earth, when Christ returns to set up His earthly kingdom.

C.I. Scofield:

The marriage supper of the Lamb is the consummation of the marriage of Christ and the Church as His bride. The figure is according to the oriental pattern of marriage covering three stages: (1) the betrothal, legally binding when the individual members of the body of Christ are saved; (2) the coming of the Bridegroom for His bride at the Rapture of the Church; and (3) the marriage supper of the Lamb, occurring in connection with the second coming of Christ to establish His millennial kingdom.[37]

19:9-10
1) Who is invited to the wedding supper of the Lamb? The O.T. and Tribulation saints, who are not part of the Bride/Church. John the Baptist (not the writer of the book of Revelation) was an Old Testament saint since he died before the Church was birthed at Pentecost. He considered himself a friend of the Bridegroom, not part of the Bride. Read John 3:26-30.

2) "The testimony of Jesus…" Read 1 John 5:11-12.

19:11-13
1) Jesus Christ, here contrasted with the First Horseman of the Apocalypse (the Antichrist, as false messiah), is also riding a white horse (Rev. 6:2).

2) The crowns Christ will be wearing are *diadema*, "the kingly ornament for the head," not *stephanos*, the crowns of reward for the saints.

3) His Name is the Word of God. Read John 1:1-3,14.

4) Christ will destroy the Antichrist with the "splendor of His coming."

Read 2 Thessalonians 2:8.

---

[37] Scofield, 1371. Notes on Revelation 19:7.

19:14-16

1) Who are the "armies of heaven"? The Bride of Christ ("dressed in fine linen, bright and clean") will be with Him, as well as the holy angels (Matt. 25:31). With them will be the souls of Old Testament saints, who were led into God's presence when Christ ascended into heaven (Ephesians 4:8-10), and the souls of the deceased Tribulation saints, all of whom will be resurrected on earth (Dan. 12:1-2; Rev. 7:9, 14, 20:4-5).

2) The imagery is that of Christ Himself treading the winepress of God's wrath. Read Rev.14:19-20, 17:14.

19:17-18

"The great supper of God" is in contrast to the wedding supper of the Lamb! This supper speaks of judgment.

19:19-21

1) The world's armies and all those who had "received the mark of the beast and worshiped his name" will be killed. These will not enter Christ's earthly kingdom, but will await the resurrection of the wicked before the great throne judgment (Rev. 20:11-15).

2) What about those still living at the time of Christ's return? Read Matthew 25:31-46. Evidence of saving faith will be the love demonstrated towards others, specifically the Jewish people ("these brothers of mine").

3) No unbeliever will enter the Millennium. Read Psalm 21:8-9.

Chapter 20: The Thousand Years and The Final Judgment

20:1-3

1) In Rev. 9:1, we saw that Satan will be given the key to the Abyss so that he can release the locust-like plague of demons. Here, a single angel will be able to cast Satan into the Abyss, locking him in.

2) Satan will be released to test those humans born during the thousand years, so that they would have an opportunity to choose Christ for themselves (Rev. 20:7-8).

20:4-6

1) Those sitting on thrones will be given authority to judge:

    a) The Church Age saints (elders sitting on thrones in Rev. 4:4) will judge the world. Read 1 Corinthians 6:1-2.

    b) The 12 apostles (part of the church, sitting on thrones) will judge the 12 tribes of Israel. Read Luke 22:28-30.

2) The "first resurrection" is the resurrection to eternal life as opposed to the resurrection of the damned (Rev. 20:11-15). ALL believers will partake in the "first resurrection," which occurs in different stages prior to the millennial reign of Christ:

    a) At the Rapture: All Church Age believers. The dead in Christ rise first (1 Thess. 4:16). Included are the living believers taken up in the Rapture, who will be "changed" (given "resurrection" bodies: 1 Cor. 15:51-55).

    b) The Two Witnesses (Just prior to Christ's return: Rev.11:7-12)

    c) At the Second Coming of Christ:

        ❖ Old Testament Saints (Dan. 12:1-3, 13)

        ❖ Also, deceased Tribulation Saints & Martyrs (Rev.20:4-6)

3) The fact that those martyred for their faith during the Tribulation period will not be resurrected until after Christ's return (Rev.20:4) tells us that the Rapture of the Church will occur before the Tribulation. If the Church were to go through the Tribulation and be raptured just prior to Christ's return (post-tribulation Rapture view) then these martyrs would be resurrected and raptured as part of the Church, prior to Christ's return.

4) A thousand years is a Millennium.

    a) Christ's Kingdom on Earth: Read Daniel 2:44.

b)   Read Isaiah 65:18-25. These will be the conditions on earth. Verse 20 speaks of longevity of life. Only unbelievers ("sinners"[38]) will die.

Note: The "first resurrection" is the believers' resurrection, and it occurs prior to the thousand-year reign of Christ. This tells us that the living believers of the Millennium period, those who enter at the start or those born during that period, will not die since there is no resurrection for believers after that point.

It appears that they will enter into eternity just as God had planned for Adam and Eve and all of humanity from the beginning. God's plans will not be thwarted. We will see more on this in Chapter 21.

5)   That only leaves the unsaved to be resurrected at the "Great White Throne Judgment" after the Millennium. We will look at that resurrection in Rev. 20:11-12. Recall our study of Hades, which tells us the souls of all the lost are still in torment until that time when their bodies will be resurrected.

20:7-10
1)   The vast number of unbelievers gathered for battle speaks of the increased world population during the thousand-year reign of Christ. The earth will continue to be populated throughout the Millennium.

2)   "Gog and Magog" is similar to the yet-future war prophesied in Ezekiel 38 and 39, where Gog is the king of the land of Magog who will come from the north and attack the land of Israel. Ezekiel speaks of an alliance of nations that will seek to invade Israel, only to be destroyed by God.

In this passage, there is also an attack against Jerusalem. However, it will come from all over the world ("four corners of the earth" = north, south, east, and west) and is led by Satan himself.

3)   The lake of burning sulfur (hell) is a place of eternal torment.

---

[38] Jamieson, Fausset, Brown. Notes on Isaiah 65:20.

20:11-12

1)   The old earth will pass away, but will be followed by the creation of the new heaven and new earth (Rev. 21:1). The White Throne Judgment of the lost seems to take place in the heavens.

2)   We saw in Rev. 20:6 that the "first resurrection" was the resurrection to eternal life.

3)   The "dead" here are all those not included in the "first resurrection." These would be the unsaved throughout history, and those who will die in the rebellion following the Millennium (Rev. 20:7-9).

4)   The unsaved will receive JUSTICE. Believers receive MERCY, through the shed blood of Jesus Christ. A believer's sins are not even remembered by God!

"I, even I, am he who blots out your transgressions, for my own sake, and remembers your sins no more" (Isaiah 43:25 NIV).

20:13-15

1)   "Death and Hades gave up their dead." Hades is now the location where the souls of the lost await final judgment.

2)   Those who reject Christ will have their names blotted out of the Book of Life. Read Psalms 9:5, 69:28; Exodus 32:31-32.

3)   The unsaved dead will be physically resurrected to face judgment. They are not annihilated; they will not cease to exist. They will be "tormented day and night forever and ever," along with Satan, the Antichrist and the False Prophet (Rev. 20:10, 15). "They perish because they refused to love the truth and so be saved" (2 Thess. 2:10).

Please refer to the detailed Revelation Timeline (p. 122) so that you can see the sequence of events. If you're a visual learner, this should be helpful.

Please refer to the Discussion Questions at the end of the lesson.

Lesson Eleven
Discussion Questions

Attention Small Group Leaders: Before proceeding to the following questions, please ask the members if there is a topic they want to discuss.

1)   What part of today's teaching was unfamiliar to you, and what did you learn today that you did not know before?

2)   What part of today's teaching was most important to you, and why?

3)   Identify the group described as "the great multitude" in the heavenly scene recorded in Rev. 19:6-8. Please also read Rev. 7:13-16, and discuss the notes for Rev. 7:11-15 in your study guide (pp. 41-42).

4)   Who is invited to "the wedding of the Lamb"? We know the Bridegroom is Jesus Christ and His Bride is the Church. Who are the invited guests? After discussing your views, please read the study guide notes for Rev. 19:9-10 (p. 107).

5)   Merriam-Webster Dictionary defines annihilationism as "the theological doctrine that the wicked will cease to exist after this life."[39] Is this biblical? Does Scripture teach the eternal damnation of the lost just as it teaches the eternal life of the believer?

Please discuss as you read Rev. 20:7-10; Rev. 14:9-11; Matthew 25:31-34, 41-46.

_____

[39]*Merriam-Webster Dictionary.*

LESSON TWELVE: CHAPTERS 21-22

◆◆◆◆

The Believer's Glorious Destiny

Overview

This lesson brings our study of end-time events to a climactic conclusion, revealing the amazing inheritance that God has prepared for His people, all because of the finished work of His only begotten Son, Jesus Christ. There will be a new heaven and a new earth, free from the defilement that mankind has brought upon God's beautiful creation.

The New Jerusalem, a satellite city, will come down out of heaven and it will be the abode of God and man together. The measurement of all sides of the city will be 1,500 miles (the approximate distance between Toronto and Miami). We are told that there will still be nations on the new earth who will walk by the light of this city. There will be no need for the sun or moon, because the glory of God will give it light, and the Lamb, Jesus Christ, will be its lamp.

There will be a River of Life flowing from the throne of God and the Lamb, down the middle of the great street of the city. On both sides of the river will be the Tree of Life, which will provide sustenance and maintain the healing of the nations. As unbelievable as it sounds, we know that it is true because these are the words of the Faithful Witness, Jesus Christ. We are told not to seal up the words of this prophecy because their fulfillment is imminent; they can occur at any time. Be ready for the coming of the Bridegroom!

21:1-2

1) The creation of the new heavens and new earth follows the judgment of the lost. <u>Read Rev. 20:11.</u>

2) Here "new" (*kainos*) means "recently made, fresh, unused, unworn." The new earth will have no oceans or seas, only dry habitable land, perhaps because the seas now divide people groups and nations. Today, over two-thirds of the earth is covered with water.

3) The Church, as the Bride of Christ, will be "beautifully dressed" in fine linen: the righteous acts of the saints (Rev. 19:8). Here, the new Jerusalem is the abode of the resurrected saints, coming down out of heaven, extravagantly prepared for God's people. The new Jerusalem is NOT the bride, but is prepared AS A BRIDE!

21:3-5

1) No more sin and death. No more resurrections are mentioned. Therefore, it appears that no one will be born on the new earth after the Millennium (in eternity) since their faith in Christ would have to be tested, as it was for those born during the Millennium. The new earth will be populated only by believers who will enter or are born during the Millennium.

2) Again, we see that the new Jerusalem is the dwelling of God AND His people—together as in the Garden of Eden (Gen. 3:8).

3) There will be no more reason for tears: no more mourning, crying, pain or death, and "the former things will not be remembered, nor will they come to mind" (Isa. 65:17).

21:6-7

1) "It is done." At Christ's crucifixion, He cried out, "It is finished," speaking of the atonement for sin. Here, it speaks of the restoration of all things.

2) Our inheritance: ALL of the saints, from all ages, will inherit everything that our heavenly Father has prepared for us.

21:8

Have you ever lied? Committed any of these others sins? Is that who you are? Read 1 Corinthians 6:11; 2 Corinthians 5:17; Romans 4:23-25.

21:9-10

1) This is the Church, not only betrothed, but now the mature spouse of Christ.

2) Again, we see the New Jerusalem descending from heaven, as the dwelling place of the Wife of the Lamb (the Church) (Rev. 3:12-13).

21:11-14

1) The city will be dazzling, reflecting the glory of God! "In my Father's house are many rooms. If it were not so, I would have told you" (John 14:2).

2) "On the gates are written the names of the twelve tribes of Israel." This is not speaking of the Church as "spiritual Israel" since the names of the Apostles, who represent the Church, are on the twelve foundations.

21:15-17

1) The new Jerusalem is described as a cube: all sides are 1,500 miles across (approx. Toronto to Miami)! The walls will be 216 feet thick.

2) J. Vernon McGee believes it to be a cube within a crystal-clear sphere, which is consistent with God's creation:

> Several times attention is called to the fact that the city is like a crystal-clear stone or crystal-clear gold. This emphasis leads us to believe that the city is seen through the crystal. We live outside the planet called earth, but the Bride will dwell within the planet called the New Jerusalem. The glory of light streaming through this crystal-clear prism, will break up into a polychromed rainbow of breath-taking beauty.[40]

---

[40] J. Vernon McGee, *Reveling Through Revelation, II* (Los Angeles: Church of the Open Door, n.d.), 104-105.

21:18-21

1)   The wall of the city was jasper (a precious gem of various colors), and each foundation will be decorated with precious stones, but the city itself will be made of pure transparent gold.

2)   Each gate is a single pearl! Each of the 12 floors (foundations) is 125 miles high (1,500 miles high divided by 12).

21:22-24

1)   Read Rev. 3:12. God Himself will be the temple. As believers, we are "in Christ."

2)   Genesis 1:3 "And God said, 'Let there be light…'" on the first day of creation. He did not create the sun and moon ("lights in the expanse of the sky to separate the day from the night") until the fourth day (1:14). God does not need the sun to produce light. Here, we see that His glory will illuminate the entire city.

3)   There will be nations (*ethnos* = "people") and kings on the new earth. Again, it appears that those living through the Millennium will populate the new earth, and have access to God in the New Jerusalem.

21:25-27

These gates will never be shut, because there will be no night (21:25). The Old Testament custom was for the city gates to be shut at night for protection, something God's people would no longer need. There will be "twelve angels at the gates" (21:12).

22:1-2

1)   There will be no sea (Rev.21:1), only the river of the water of life. "River" comes from the root word *pino*, which means "figuratively, to receive into the soul what serves to refresh, strengthen it, nourish it unto eternal life."

2)   Where have we seen the "tree of life" in previous Scripture passages? The tree of life was first seen in the Garden of Eden. Read Gen. 2:9, 3:21-24.

God did not want man to live forever in his sinful condition, and so prevented Adam and Eve from eating of the tree of life.

In Revelation 21, we have seen that because of what God's Son, Jesus Christ, has accomplished on our behalf, man will live with God forever in a sinless condition. It appears that the millennial saints, those who will not die but will survive the Tribulation period and enter into Christ's thousand-year reign on earth, as well as believers born during the Millennium, will populate the new earth. They will have access to the New Jerusalem (God's satellite city whose "gates will never be shut").

Could it be that God's original plan for man in the Garden of Eden will yet be fulfilled on earth? Yes, and more: His Son will have a wife (the Church), and they will be joined by resurrected Old Testament and Tribulation Saints, as they dwell in the New Jerusalem.

In the book of Revelation, we see that God is finishing what was started in Genesis. He is demonstrating that even while preserving man's free will, He is sovereign and controls the outcome of human history. No plan of His can be thwarted.

22:3-5

"The curse came upon those in Paradise on account of their sins. There shall be no more curse, for no sin shall ever enter the New Jerusalem."[41]

22:6-7

1) Prophecy (*propheteia*) is a "discourse emanating from divine inspiration and declaring the purposes of God, whether by reproving and admonishing the wicked, or comforting the afflicted, or revealing things hidden; esp. by foretelling future events."

2) "Behold, I am coming soon" (Jesus is now speaking, not the angel). "Soon" (*tachos*) means "quickness, speed." When it happens, it will happen quickly, suddenly, beginning with the Rapture of the Church.

---

[41] Johnson. *People's New Testament.* Notes on Revelation 22:3.

3) To "keep" (*tereo*) is to "heed, to attend to carefully." We are not to dismiss the prophecies of this book, but to take them seriously. Live like you believe it!

22:8-9
Matthew 4:10 "...worship the Lord your God, and serve Him only."

22:10-11
1) To "seal" (*sphragizo*) is "to hide, keep in silence, keep secret." Here, do not seal up!

2) "The time is near."

    a) "Time" (*kairos*) is a "period of time."

    b) "Near" (*engus*) is "imminent" (ready to take place at any time).

3) Let him who does wrong continue... It is their choice.

Read Daniel 12:10.

22:12-13
1) A "reward" (*misthos*) is "wages earned; of the rewards which God bestows, or will bestow, on good deeds and endeavors."

2) Rewards are what is due for the works done in this life. They are in addition to salvation, which <u>cannot</u> be earned (Eph. 2:8-9). Church Age believers receive crowns of reward at the Rapture. We see them (us) seated on thrones with their crowns in Chapter 4.

22:14-15
1) The lost are still in existence (not annihilated); but exist outside of God's presence in the fiery lake of burning sulfur—hell (21:8).

2) A "dog" (*kuon*) as used here is "metaphorically, a man of impure mind, an impudent man."

22:16-17

1) A church (*ekklesia*) is an "assembly of Christians." While this letter was originally addressed to the seven local churches, the message is for all Christians of all time. "The Spirit and the bride say, 'Come!'" (22:17). The bride is the entire Church!

2) The invitation of the Holy Spirit and of the Bride of Christ, His Church, is to all: "Whoever is thirsty...whoever wishes, let him take the free gift of the water of life."

22:18-19

This passage does not refer to differences in interpretation. Satan would love for us to stay away from this book for fear that we would misinterpret it. Remember, there is a blessing to all who read, and hear, and take to heart the words of this prophecy (Rev. 1:3).

We must handle the Word of God reverently, and prayerfully pursue the study of God's Word under the teaching of the Holy Spirit.

Final Passage:

22:20-21

1) Here, the invitation is to the Lord: "Come, Lord Jesus." Read 2 Tim. 4:8.

2) "Grace" (*charis*) means "goodwill, loving kindness, favor."

3) "Lord" (*kurios*) is defined as "the owner; one who has control of the person, the master."

As we conclude this study of the book of Revelation and end-time prophecies, please know that...*You are blessed!*

"Blessed is the one who reads the words of this prophecy, and blessed are those who hear it and take to heart what is written in it, because the time is near" (Rev.1:3 NIV).

As you've immersed yourself in God's Word, not only in the book of Revelation, but throughout the Scriptures, you have seen God's wonderful plan and provision for mankind. He sent His one and only Son to pay the penalty for our sins. "For it is by grace you have been saved, through faith—and this not from yourselves, it is the gift of God—not by works, so that no one can boast" (NIV).

It is not enough to believe *about* Jesus. We need a one-on-one transaction with Him, when—by faith—we give Him our sin and receive His righteousness; when we give Him our lives and receive His life. We place our trust in Him.

Who do you say Jesus Christ is? Are you a true believer in Christ?
Or are you merely an unsaved church member?

If you have never trusted Christ as your personal Savior, asking for His forgiveness, you can pray this prayer of faith right now—and He will receive you as His own:

Lord Jesus, I believe that You are the only begotten Son of God, that You are fully God and fully human. I believe that You led a sinless life and that You died on the cross for the sins of the world—including mine. I believe that God the Father, by the power of the Holy Spirit, raised You from the dead and that You will come again to judge the living and the dead. I ask you to forgive me and save me so that I can be reconciled with my Heavenly Father, be filled with the Holy Spirit, and live with You forever. I receive You as the Lord of my life and the master of my soul. In Christ's Name, I pray. Amen.

If you have received Christ's death as payment for your sins, and personally trusted Him as your Savior, then you are God's possession, purchased by the blood of Christ. But does He have *control* of you?

Are you surrendered to His Lordship in YOUR life?

"And he died for all, that those who live should no longer live for themselves but for him who died for them and was raised again" (2 Corinthians 5:15).

Let's join together in a prayer for a renewed dedication of our lives:

Lord God, I confess that I have gone my own way and leaned upon my own understanding. I have allowed the world to lure me away from obedience and surrender to You, and I have allowed Satan to deceive me in many ways. But I trust in Your mercy and in Your power to enable me to live the life You've called me to live "in Christ." I ask You, Father, in the Name of the LORD Jesus Christ, and by the power of His Blood, to turn my eyes from worthless things; renew my life according to your Word. Amen!

Please refer to the Discussion Questions at the end of the lesson.

7 Seals of Judgment of the Earth (Rev. 6)
1st Seal: First Horseman (Antichrist)
2nd Seal: Second Horseman (War)
3rd Seal: Third Horseman (Famine)
4th Seal: Fourth Horseman (Death)
5th Seal: Souls of Martyrs Under Altar
6th Seal: Cataclysmic Natural Event

Announcement of Great Tribulation (Rev. 6:17)

The 7th Seal (8:1) covers the final 3-1/2 years of the Great Tribulation including:
     7 Trumpets of Judgment
     7 Bowls of God's Wrath

Battle of Armageddon (Rev. 16:12-16)

Resurrection of O.T. Saints (Dan. 12:1-3)
Resurrection of Tribulation Saints (Rev. 20:4)

Surviving Tribulation Saints enter the Millennium on earth and continue bearing children (Isa. 65:19-23).

Church Age	PENTECOST: Birth of the Church (Acts 2) Revelation Chapters 2 & 3 Rapture of the Church (I Thess.4)		
7-Year Tribulation	**Divine Plan of Grace & Salvation**	First Half of Tribulation: 3-1/2 years	**Revelation Chapters 4-19 / The Church in Heaven**
		Great Tribulation: 3-1/2 years	
Millennium	Return of Christ with His Bride (Rev. 19:8, 11-14)		
	Satan bound during Thousand Year Reign of Christ on earth. (Rev. 20: 1-3)		
Satan released to test those born during 1,000 years. Unbelievers rebel and are destroyed. (Rev. 20:7-10)			
White Throne Judgement of the Lost (Rev. 20:11-15)			
Eternity	New Heaven and New Earth (Rev. 21:1) New Jerusalem as satellite City of God above the earth (Rev. 21:2, 22-27) ETERNAL STATE: All believers having access to the presence of Almighty God! (Rev. 22)		

Lesson Twelve
Discussion Questions

Attention Small Group Leaders: Before proceeding to the following questions, please ask the members if there is a topic they want to discuss.

1)   What part of today's teaching was unfamiliar to you, and what did you learn today that you did not know before?

2)   What part of today's teaching was most important to you, and why?

3)   The account of the "tree of life" begins in Genesis and ends here in Revelation 22. The Lord our God will bring human history full circle. Please read and discuss Rev. 22:1-2 and the corresponding notes in the study guide (pp. 116-117).

4)   Rev. 22:14-15 shows the parallel existence of those who dwell with God, and the lost who will live forever outside of God's Presence. The judgment of the lost may appear to be cruel, yet God has made every provision through His Son, Jesus Christ, for their salvation.

   ❖ Please read Rev. 22:14-17 and discuss the profound consequences of rejecting the grace of God.

   ❖ Please read and discuss Romans 1:18-20; 2 Thess. 1:5-10 and 2:9-10.

   ❖ Should people have the free will to choose to receive or reject God's free gift of eternal life? Why or why not?

5)   How has the study of the book of Revelation affected the way you view God's Word, your relationships with other believers, and your concern to reach unsaved people with the Gospel of Jesus Christ?

BIBLIOGRAPHY

Anderson, Sir Robert. *The Coming Prince: The Last Great Monarch of Christendom.* London: Hodder and Stoughton, 1881.

Easton, Matthew George. *Easton's Bible Dictionary*, 1897. Public domain.

Henry, Matthew. *Commentary on the Whole Bible,* 1706. Public domain.

Jamieson, Robert, A.R. Fausset and David Brown. *Commentary Critical and Explanatory on the Whole Bible*, 1871. Public domain.

Johnson, Barton W. *People's New Testament*, 1891. Public domain.

McGee, J. Vernon. *Exodus Volume II.* Pasadena: Thru the Bible Books, 1975.

_____. *Notes & Outlines: Daniel.* Pasadena, CA: Thru the Bible Radio.

_____. *Reveling Through Revelation, II.* Pasadena: Thru the Bible Books, 1979.

Miriam-Webster Dictionary © 1997 by Miriam-Webster, Incorporated.

Scofield, C.I. ed. *The New Scofield Reference Bible: Authorized King James Version.* New York: Oxford University Press, 1967.

Smith, William. *Smith's Bible Dictionary*, 1901. Public domain.

Walvoord, John F. *The Revelation of Jesus Christ.* Chicago: Moody Press, 1966.

Made in United States
Orlando, FL
08 April 2022